D1298927

People-Smart Leaders Measure Behavior Change

If you are looking to implement a program that will take you from where you are to where you really want to be, let me suggest to you that you've come to the right place. I highly recommend this approach and have implemented it in our organization and am pleased with the higher level of productivity and expectations coming from all levels of our company.

Roger Cox, CEO, Arkansas Utility Protection Services

I found the concept of measuring the effectiveness of behaviors that influence working relationships to be right on target for improving overall organizational effectiveness. Just as we measure KPIs on the plant floor to assess our operational efficiencies, we should learn to measure "people KPIs" to assess our "people efficiencies."

**James Young, Vice President, Production Services,
Tyson Foods, Inc.**

The authors of this book were right on with developing a way to measure people performance. We always measure the technical side of the business. Why not measure the people side of the business to improve working relationships?

Jeff Power, Complex Manager, Tyson Foods, Inc.

Knowledge has no practical value unless engrained in our daily routines. *People-Smart Leaders* provides a systematic process to improve interpersonal performance and working relationships.

Jerry Vest, President, Regions Bank Northwest Arkansas

Are you ready to enter The People Age? Then this is the book to guide you to a more people-centered, sustainable, and measured approach to lasting change. These authors have given us a balanced, proven process for developing workplace values and behaviors with tools to measure performance, provide accountability, and ensure success.

Ed Rosenberg, President, Positioned 2 Soar

Bookshelves are lined with material that stresses the importance and impact of social values in the workplace. The authors give you guidance for understanding and identifying these values while showing you the tools to measure and monitor those behavior changes. The book is a must-read for anyone truly interested in improving employee relationships in the workplace.

Richard Meshell, Human Resources Manager, Teris, LLC

This book strikes at the heart of where organizations struggle the most: integrating its people into the process of performance excellence. It is practical, insightful, and challenging. In today's rapidly changing business landscape, business as usual just won't do. Thanks for a tool to help foster real and lasting change.

Terry Nichols, Plant Manager, Allen Family Foods

These authors provide an excellent roadmap to develop working relationships along with a measurement system to track progress that will certainly return dollars to the financial bottom line.

Duffy McKenzie, Chief Operating Officer, Choctaw Maid Farms, Inc.

This book captures the thinking that surrounds popular literature while adding new perspectives from a systematic approach. This book defines the importance of developing the system that will be used as a model for one's business leadership. The system then holds the leadership accountable in following that team model.

Rick Izor, General Manager, Scroll Technologies

The authors provide a very straightforward, comprehensible, and immediately applicable blueprint for making organizations more effective and productive. They focus on the key to success for organizations seeking to make the leap to the true high-performance frontier—*people.*

Mary Aleese Schreiber, President, Stafford Management Group

These authors have developed a tangible and measurable system for evaluating and improving working relationships, a critical component of any leader's success. Great reading to evaluate any organization.

Craig Young, President, United Holding Company, Inc.

We all know that large-scale change requires a significant amount of change from a number of people in the organization, not just a few. These authors introduce a unique and highly useful methodology to quantify the behavioral characteristics of working relationships in real time. The feedback generated is critical in driving long-term behavior and cultural change.

Bo Thomas, Ph.D., Coauthor, *The Real Dream Team: Seven Practices Used by World-Class Team Leaders to Achieve Extraordinary Results*

People-Smart Leaders clearly and powerfully illustrates the everyday, on-the-job situations that any employee can relate to and recognize.

Dennis S. Reina, Ph.D., Coauthor, *Trust & Betrayal in the Workplace: Rebuilding Effective Relationships in Your Organization*

It is a real pleasure to read a book that provides in a manner that is reader friendly such important information about how to improve interpersonal performance. The content of this book is both informative and applicable to improving the organization's performance.

Reggie Corbitt, CEO, Little Rock Wastewater Utility

This book provides the blueprint that increases the probability that positive change will occur within an organization as well as encourage change to occur in the future.

Ron Schoo, Technical Development Manager, Cargill Pork

These authors offer practical tools to tapping your people resource and enhancing profits. They provide solid direction on how to enhance the performance of your people without having to pay more to get it.

Jerry Wilson, President, Jerry Wilson & Associates, LLC

People-Smart Leaders offers well-researched and thought-provoking content. Managers who want to be better leaders and to improve performance should implement the people systems outlined in this book.

Paul Phillips, President, Paul Phillips & Associates, Inc.

The authors have produced an accessible means for managers interested in identifying and implementing a values-based strategy for working with people in organizations. Most important, *People-Smart Leaders* offers a practical, effective means for addressing the human problems associated with change in contemporary organizations.

Hubert S. Field, Ph.D., Torchmark Professor of Management, Auburn University

People-Smart Leaders is packed with practical methods that will help leaders in organizations that are performing below expectations to transform the potential of an organization's human resources into a high-performance organization.

Achilles Armenakis, DBA, Pursell Professor of Management, Auburn University

This book raises the bar for organizational leaders to continuously improve the efficiency of their human capital by measuring the dynamics of interpersonal performance of working relationships in real time.

John Elizandro, Vice President, Villanova University

These authors do for corporate communities what Stephen Covey did for the individual. They provide a roadmap for identifying where you are with your people, help you determine where you want to go, and then do not leave you hanging there. The next step is giving a system of true follow-up to track your "people progress."

Brian Curry, American Express

I once worked with a plant that spent $40 million on equipment and hiring and training employees to operate the equipment. Very little money was spent on their people capital, and this plant lost over $10 million per year for over five years. If they had used the principles in this book, this plant would certainly have been millions of dollars ahead by now.

Bill Verwolf, General Manager, Smurfit-Stone Container Corporation

The strength of an organization is its people. The strength of a leader is to recognize that. These authors show us how to become successful leader and to build organizations that will consider the human and social side of corporate life. It is a must-read for anyone who supervises people at any level.

John Bekkers, President & CEO, Gold Kist, Inc.

These authors have armed management with new insight to develop the company's most important asset—its people. I need to have my managers read this book before my competitors do.

Rick Schultz, President & CEO, Spectrum Surgical Instruments Corporation

This book is right on target for today's environment. With breakthrough insights on the how-to's of being a People Smart Leader, it is precisely what forward-thinking business leaders need to know.

Eric Hutchinson, CFP, Chairman, Hutchinson/Ifrah Financial Services, Inc.

People-Smart Leaders is a refreshing new look at how to improve working relationships by applying a simple three-step process. Managers finally have a method and the tool to change the specific behaviors that improve working relationships among team members.

James Marbury, Plant Manager, Entergy, White Bluff Plant

People-Smart Leaders

Larry Cole, Ph.D.
Michael S. Cole, Ph.D.

Oak Hill Press
Winchester, Virginia

Printed in the United States of America
Jacket design by Michael Komarck
Text design by Bookwrights

Library of Congress Cataloging-in-Publication Data
Cole, Larry, 1945-
  People-smart leaders : maximizing people, performance, and profits / by
    Larry Cole & Michael Cole ; foreword by Ray Pelletier.
    p. cm.
  Includes index.
  ISBN 1-886939-61-6 (alk. paper)
  1. Teams in the workplace--Management. 2. Industrial management--
    Social aspects. 3. Organizational effectiveness. 4. Leadership. I. Cole,
    Michael, 1973- II. Title.
  HD66.C537 2004
  658.3'145--dc22   2004053153

Oakhill Press
1647 Cedar Grove Road
Winchester, VA 22603
800-32-books

Contents

Foreword

Wow! After reading *People-Smart Leaders* you are going to wonder why did it take someone so long to write this book? For 30 years I have worked in business and the military, and I'm excited to be able to recommend this book to all my clients so they can use this work as a powerful and easy to use "blueprint." This well-written and real-world book is practical and will give them gems of knowledge to help them increase sales, improve teamwork, and improve customer service and the bottom line.

Larry and Michael speak to the heart of successful organizations—people working together. Furthermore they focus your attention upon the efficiency of three working relationships:

1. How members of the teams and department work together as a unit.
2. The supervisor or team leader's impact upon the efficiency of the working relationship.
3. And, between departments or teams.

The authors are in-demand speakers and consultants who truly understand business; they don't just write about business, they live it. They advance the notion of defining the performance parameters that you'll want to guide you and your organization in the efficiency of your working relationships in a manner similar to how the processes are defined to guide the technical success. Leaders such as yourself cannot afford to leave the definition of your crucial technical measurements to chance or, worse yet, to the whim of one's personality for the obvious reason that doing so would lead to the demise of the organization. You will learn how to apply this same business sense to the interpersonal behaviors that essentially serve as the engine that drives efficient and positive working relationships.

This book has changed and helped me in measuring the soft skills (you'll also read that the authors discourage the use of this term). Like many people, I didn't think it could be done easily. Not only will you learn about how it can be done to monitor the efficiency of the three basic working relationships, but you'll be encouraged to use this practical tool on a regular basis to improve performance as you monitor the numbers associated with the technical parameters to guide success.

I don't want to steal the authors' thunder, but I want to forewarn you that you will be introduced to many concepts that will challenge your thinking. For example, *"I'm guilty until I prove my innocence," "My success is helping you to be successful,"* and *"Your perception of me is more important than my perception of me!"*

I know you'll enjoy this book, and it will help you and your organization work together effectively, efficiently, and positively.

Ray Pelletier, CSP, CPAE
"America's Leadership Advisor"
Author of the business bestseller, *Permission to Win*
Member of the "Speakers Hall of Fame"

Acknowledgments

First and foremost, the authors want to thank those clients that have helped us pioneer the TeamMax® teambuilding process over the past decade. Sometimes without fully understanding the ramifications of the TeamMax® processes, these clients took a leap of faith to try something they questioned could be done—measure people performance. This book is a product of that work, so in reality these clients are responsible for giving us the knowledge to share with you. Working with our clients to maximize their people capital was also the stimulus that pushed the development of measuring people performance in real time and the birth of the MBC Software® methodology.

Second, we want to thank Ed Helvey, Publisher, and Dae Scott, Production Editor, at Oakhill Press for their assistance and guidance to make this book a reality. Without going into detail, this book is an example that persistence pays off, and Ed recognized the value of this book and agreed that it needed to be published to share with you.

Third, not many parents have the pleasure of writing a book with one of their children as I have had the privilege to coauthor this book with my son, Michael. This will always be a special memory.

Preface

A company exists to make a profit. Profit is the direct result of people working together to produce a product or service. Thanks to Daniel Goleman and his best-selling series of books on emotional intelligence, a heightened awareness now exists of how people within corporate workplace environments work with each other.

While Goleman's work has had a very important and positive impact, other authors have written about the importance of workplace social behaviors. James O'Toole in his book *Leading Change* encouraged the reader to adopt what he referred to as the Rushmorean values of integrity, trust, listening, and respect. Rob Lebow and William Simon discussed eight values (truth, trust, mentoring, openness, risk-taking, giving credit, honesty, and caring) in their book *Lasting Change.* The best-selling book, *First, Break All the Rules: What the World's Greatest Managers Do Differently,* by Marcus Buckingham and Curt Coffman crossed the measurement threshold and offered twelve very specific behaviors that can be measured. Additionally these authors present convincing evidence that the impact of these behaviors upon production can likewise be measured.

Why This Book Is Needed

The missing link in the discussions about the importance of social values in the workplace is *a process to measure and monitor the use of the behaviors contained within each value.* The success of every organization is based on the efficiency of three working relationships, which we have labeled the "people operating system." These three working relationships are those among members of the work unit, between members of the work unit and their supervisor, and between work units.

In this book, you learn a blueprint for defining the desired teamwork social values in terms of behaviors that can be seen, taught, repeated, and measured. *We are introducing a measurement methodology that allows you to quantify the use of the desired behaviors within these three working relationships in real time.* In doing so, you can define and measure the implementation of behavioral solutions to improve teamwork as you measure the impact of solutions to improve technical performance.

People Problems Are Stealing Money

The hallways and work areas in every organization echo with complaints about frustrations and toxicity in working relationships. Most organizational leaders allow this unbridled energy to act like an undetected virus that erodes morale and production as if the organization were a helpless victim. This erosion takes money from the bottom line. If leaders developed their manufacturing or service delivery systems in the same blind manner as they develop their people assets, their business would be a blur of chaos and confusion.

Employees in our research base estimate that frustrations in working relationships caused by people problems reduce the organizational efficiency in the three working relationships by as much as 30 percent. That translates into a whopping loss of two-and-a-half hours out of every eight-hour workday.

At the same time that these frustrations are stealing money from the bottom line, the corporate battle cry to increase performance grows louder. The push is on to boost profits through greater productivity, reducing the number of employees, and other strategic strategies. Organizational leaders eagerly measure and monitor a stream of technical characteristics in anticipation of their success. Increased performance, however, requires that people do a better job of working together. As a matter of fact, actions such as openly communicating, cooperating, trusting, and respecting each other determine the success of people working together. Yet, the use of these behaviors is not measured!

The fact that the very issues that determine the success of every organization are neither regularly measured nor monitored is analogous to a railroad company only maintaining one rail of a railroad track. The train will ultimately derail. To succeed, high-performing organizations must take care of both the tracks that compose their organization: their people and the technical characteristics.

If organizational leaders are really intent on maximizing profitability, then why does this asymmetry—emphasizing technical characteristics over people-based processes—continue? Actually, several potential hypotheses explain the lack of attention given to continuously improving the organization's people performance. The time has come to apply a systematic process to enter into the "people age."

Words, of course, must be converted into action. However, people resist change because of the associated consequences. Five sources of resistance frequently kill organizational change efforts. This book offers a detailed blueprint on how to apply ten strategies to successfully lead the change effort through the minefields of resistance associated with each of the five stages of organizational change. In doing so, you learn that resistance is actually a friend rather than a foe of the change process.

We believe that by the time you finish reading this book you will agree that the bar has been raised with the introduction of a comprehensive, systematic process to develop people capital through quantifying behavior change.

Introduction

You are going to learn about a comprehensive measurement system to monitor and improve people performance. People constitute the engine that drives the technical performance and financial success of your company. Without people working together, you would not have a company.

Our research has shown that organizations lose 25 to 30 percent of their efficiency because of people-related problems. Convert that inefficiency to dollars, and you can quickly ascertain that about 25 percent of your operating budget is walking out the door every day. This drain on financial resources has become just another integral element of the organization's comfort zone and an expected cost of doing business. We think you will agree that it is time to stop the financial waste. We are offering you a solution to improve people performance and thus improve the efficiency of your people operating systems to put more profit into your stakeholders' pockets.

Traditionally, the emphasis has been on measuring technical performance for a variety of reasons, which we discuss in this book. You are about to learn a systematic process to improve interpersonal performance in the three working relationships that are contained within the people operating systems which determine the technical and financial success of your company. We have labeled the process TeamMax® to emphasize the focus on improving teamwork—the people processes. The TeamMax® process to measure the "people" components of the success formula is patterned after the proven processes to measure and monitor technical success. Combining both measurement systems gives your company a comprehensive measurement system to monitor and guide the organizational health of your company.

People-Smart Leaders contains five parts.

Part One: Human Factor. The first three chapters address people issues that are costing your organization money. Part 1 asks you to evaluate your commitment to do whatever it takes to improve the people performance within your company.

Part Two: People Systems. The next five chapters address the basic elements of the TeamMax® team building process—specifically, the people operating systems and the challenges that must be addressed when using numbers to monitor and guide the people side of your company. The people operating systems consist of the three working relationships that drive the company's success:

1. Among members of a work unit.
2. Between employees and their supervisor.
3. Between work units.

Part Three: Change. Chapters 9 through 11 provide a comprehensive blueprint to effectively manage the energy systems inherent in the change process. In doing so, you learn the reasons that resistance to change can either be a friend or foe of the change process. You learn how to use this important energy source to propel change. The lack of accountability is often the culprit that sabotages change efforts, and we address the three levels of accountability and introduce a seven-step personal change process to exhibit personal accountability.

Part Four: Personal Development. We understand the cliché that "the word 'teamwork' doesn't have an 'I'." However, each employee is required to make an "I" decision to be a high-performing member of the team. To be a high-performing individual and to maximize your people resources, you must know who you are. Chapters 12 and 13 address important personal requirements and offer a process to improve personal performance to be a high-performing team member.

Part Five: Leading You into Tomorrow. In reality the workplace is a university for learning effective interpersonal skills and giving ample opportunities to work with a variety of challenging individuals. Chapters 14 through 16 discuss taking advantage of the workplace environment to maximize personal effectiveness and an easy-to-use model to help learn the necessary self-discipline to improve personal performance. The final chapter raises the question of using people operating systems to underwrite the future success of your organization.

Part One
HUMAN FACTOR

1 | Frustration Is Your Best Friend®

Frustrations in working relationships cost your company a lot of money. Do you know how much? Employees and managers have estimated that they lose as much as 30 percent of their efficiency because of the frustrations that people cause with each other.

Corporate hallways buzz with stories about communication breakdowns, lack of cooperation, the use of ineffective interpersonal skills, and other frustrations in the working relationships.

"We hurry up and then have to wait until we receive the needed information from the sales department."

"Why doesn't somebody do something about the fact that the engineering department's failure to meet deadlines is adversely impacting all of us?"

"We meet and agree what needs to be done, but nothing changes. That meeting becomes a complete waste of time. They knew nothing would change in the first place."

"Our supervisor acts as if all of us are dummies."

"The next time that person screams at me during the telephone conversation, I'm going to hang up. It will be a cold summer day before we cooperate with him."

"Everyone knows that she seems to enjoy making life more difficult for all of us. How does she keep her employment?"

More disturbing than the stories themselves is the expectation that this frustration is the normal way for corporate life, that is it has always been that way and history determines the future. We're teaching people that such inefficiency is acceptable.

Not talked about much is the fact that every interruption in work efficiency costs money.

The scenario becomes even more perplexing upon considering that organizational leaders and shareholders quickly state that their organization exists to make money, which is evidenced by the push to increase profits through more efficient production, employee reductions, product mix, and improved customer satisfaction. Organizational leaders know the precise cost to produce each component or deliver a unit of service. The cost of a service interruption or a given machine going off-line is calculated to the penny. Every effort is made to ensure production and that service delivery systems operate at 100 percent efficiency.

Here's the irony. While every effort is made to improve the efficiency of the systems underlying the technical aspects of producing a product or delivering a service, ineffective working relationships steal profits from the bottom line. With 30 percent inefficiency, almost two-and-a-half hours of each eight-hour day are lost because of frustrations in working relationships. Think in terms of money. With a 30 percent inefficiency, thirty cents of each dollar of your operating budget is stolen. Do the math with your overall operating budget. Do you like that number?

Yes, people problems are silent thieves stealing money from the financial bottom line. While one hand is doing everything possible to improve profitability, the other hand is throwing money away. Improving interpersonal effectiveness and working relationships may in fact represent a lucrative opportunity to improve profits.

Can Frustration Really Be a Friend?

The title of this chapter, "Frustration Is Your Best Friend," is not a contradiction. Ask yourself the following questions:

Do you want to be considered mediocre?

Do you want to remain complacent?

Do you want to be considered average, knowing full well that average is the best of the least and the least of the best?

Our guess is that you have answered at least one, if not all, of these questions with a resounding NO! If so, then you're ready to learn how to become best friends with frustration.

Remember the proverbial frog story? Place a frog in a pot of hot water and what will the frog do? Jump out to escape the pain. But place that same frog in a pot of cold water and begin warming it ever so slowly. What will the frog do this time? It will become acclimated, ignoring the rising temperature of the water until it's too late. The frog, comfortable to the end, will die.

Remember that you've been swimming around in the ruts of your routines, through the halls of your organization, for quite some time. The temperature may be reaching the danger point without your being aware of it. Remember also that the difference between a rut and a grave is the depth. The caution in this truism is that you must choose your ruts carefully, as they can quickly become graves. How many people escape from graves?

Consider two more questions:

Have you ever been frustrated?

Did you enjoy it?

Now do you see the problem? All of us have been frustrated and, no, we didn't like it. Frustration is uncomfortable, so the natural tendency is to avoid it. Ignoring frustration, however, can kill your personal and career development and ultimately seal the coffin in which your organization will be placed.

Understand that *frustration is your friend*®, a signal that something must be improved. Instead of ignoring frustration, we encourage you to embrace it. Seek it out. If it is costing your organization 30 percent of your efficiency, frustration needs to be more than your friend. You need to live with it in an effort to minimize its impact. In the subsequent chapters, we even show you a process to measure the degree of frustration.

Frustration As the Fuel for Change

Consider that you continue doing what you have always done until you become dissatisfied with the outcome. Every bad habit you have ever changed continued to be habit until you made a conscious decision: "I cannot continue living like this." At that point in time, you mustered the energy to climb out of the rut of your routines and begin the process of change.

I remember as if it were yesterday: being a thirty-year-old former athlete and suddenly finding that I couldn't jog around the block without having to stop, rest, and catch my breath. The realization that I was so terribly out of shape was disturbing, but it was also the beginning of a very beneficial lifestyle change. At that precise moment, frustration was my friend.

Dissatisfaction or frustration with the status quo plays the same role in your corporate life: the energy source that propels change.

Consider any piece of equipment—a car, for example. When the brakes on your car begin to make an awful screeching noise, they are talking to you, telling you that something needs to change. At that point you have a decision to make: continue to drive regardless of the (possibly hazardous) condition of your brakes, or rectify the situation by buying new brake pads.

Better yet, consider the screeching of a machine on the production line. The machine is shouting, "Pay attention to me or you'll be sorry, because I'll get into your pocketbook." Screeching, malfunctioning, and error messages are the only languages machines speak. Because the revenue stream is important, the machine receives immediate attention.

People also make noise when something is wrong. The frustration associated with difficulties and breakdowns in workplace relationships usually takes the form of verbalizing—griping and complaining, moaning and groaning. These signals usually indicate that something needs to be changed or improved.

For example, think of team members who complain about an overcontrolling work unit leader who insists on personally approving every decision affecting the group, no matter how minor. You can imagine the consequences of the frustration these people feel at not being considered competent to make decisions and at the logjams that occur while waiting for approval by the micromanaging leader. In this case, the frustration expressed signals that this work unit leader needs to exhibit more trust and to empower her employees.

Consider the frustration expressed by a group of senior managers because their plant manager does not treat them fairly. The plant manager had actually stated that some of his staff had more important roles than others—in particular, he said that engineering, quality, and even safety took a back seat to production and maintenance! The frustration expressed was a signal for the need to change, in this case to ensure that all team members—and the work of the groups for which they were responsible—be treated as equal and significant contributors to the success of the plant.

If the employees in these examples lacked the opportunity to express their frustration openly, had complained only to each other, the opportunity to improve the working relationships in their respective workplaces would have been lost. They would have continued to suffer individually, and their companies would have suffered as well, in terms of the lowered productivity that inevitably results from poor morale.

Changing the Paradigm

The preceding examples raise a crucial point about the human, social side of corporate life—the importance of creating an environment in which people feel comfortable expressing their opinions and frustrations. The time has come to change our thinking. Traditionally, expressing frustration about working relationships has been perceived as petty griping and moaning, not welcomed and definitely not encouraged. But if we can learn to see frustration as a signal that change is needed, we can seize the opportunities for making improvements that can benefit the organization.

In Closing

Our position is quite simple. Just as the screeching machine demands attention, so do screeching human beings. Frustrations in the workplace cost money in a variety of silent ways: time involved in griping, redoing work that another person/department should have completed, low morale, production slowdowns, and general inefficiencies. We think you will agree with the necessity of reducing this drain on the financial bottom line. It's time to harness this energy source and channel it to a more productive and profitable outcome.

Who said the ugly duckling couldn't grow to be a beautiful swan?

2 | Why Is the Work in Teamwork Not Working?

After all that has been written about the importance of teamwork in corporate America, why do so many efforts to improve teamwork behavior and the working relationship continue to fail for many corporate communities? Chauncy Hare and Judith Wyatt reported a surprising statistic in their book *Work Abuse:* 95 percent of today's managers continue to practice autocratic, dictatorial behaviors in a world that talks teamwork. These findings stem from research involving more than one thousand work groups.

Walk the halls of most organizations, and you'll hear stories of individuals being unable to work together, oftentimes causing tensions between all employees, resulting in the work unit failing to reach its goals or objectives. These stories typically have at least one of three common themes. The first tells the tale of work units that work with their own agenda instead of successfully cooperating with their internal customers. The second revolves around work unit leaders who use behaviors that adversely impact the working relationship with their employees. The third describes individuals who are engaging in interpersonal skills that make it difficult for their colleagues to work with them.

As you ponder the behaviors used to adversely impact working relationships, one has to wonder if walking through the company doorway somehow strips people of common sense. People inside organizations tend to act as if they regarded one another as enemies rather than as working for the same company. The survival-of-the-fittest mentality seems to drive people to compete with one another rather than understand that the organization's success depends upon cooperation, not competition. The mystery deepens when we consider the generally accepted fact that the power of people working *together* creates a successful organization. Without people working together, there is no organization—only the shell of the building and equipment. People working together determine the success of every organization, so why would anyone agree on the importance of teamwork, yet do little if anything to ensure its success?

To say the least, the failure to implement effective working relationships is depressing and begs an important question: "Does the failure to implement true teamwork behaviors mean that corporate leaders are unable to learn, or are other forces operating?" We know the answer to that question at the micro level. People are not changing. The irony is that we live at a time when some changes are occurring at warp speed. Technological innovations surfacing in the marketplace today become obsolete tomorrow. Mergers, buyouts, and organizational reconfiguration instigate change faster than we can assimilate it. A manager recently talked about being assigned the task of integrating the technical systems of a newly purchased company into his own international company. During his first meeting with the acquired corporation, he learned that his own company was being purchased by another conglomerate. His comment: "You must be able to manage change in order to survive in this jungle."

In spite of all this rapid change, the culture to systematically improve working relationships hits a brick wall. Why are we so seemingly effective at implementing change in the technical arena and so pitiful in improving the efficiency of working relationships?

Let's explore five factors contributing to the root causes of this dilemma.

1. *Why is effective teamwork not practiced?* Despite all the nice-sounding words to the contrary, teamwork is forgotten and is clearly not a priority.

"Getting the job done" sets the rules for the day. The prevailing mindset is that producing a product or delivering a service is the only immediate priority. Consequently, the focus is on specific technical responsibilities to manufacture a product, deliver a service, and post good numbers. The specific agenda for the work unit takes precedence over helping internal customers or other departments to likewise be successful. Teamwork not being a priority is particularly telling when the technical alligators are snapping, yet that is precisely when the need for teamwork is crucial. In the words of Eric Broden, author of *Hitting Below the Belt,* "Do you think those poor souls on the *Titanic* practiced good teamwork? They just wanted off the ship." Maybe with a little more teamwork, more people would have made it safely off the *Titanic* and into the boats?

A young training manager complaining about the lack of teamwork recently said, "The words used to train people on how to work together more effectively sound good today, but are lost tomorrow when the employee returns to the warfare mentality of our organization." Unfortunately, he is right. Teamwork training does very little if any good when the culture does not support the behaviors included in the training program.

2. *Why is teamwork forgotten?* Being profitable is the reason your company exists. Emblazoned in the minds of leaders is the predominant thought that the technical side of the organization—producing a product or delivering services—is the real revenue generator. Watch the frantic

efforts to improve the performance of a machine operating at 70 percent capacity, because the revenue stream becomes severely affected. It is imperative to keep the money faucet flowing at a steady stream.

These same leaders may agree with the organizational truism that the financial success of producing a product or delivering a service depends upon people working together. Consequently, the real money generators in the organization are people and their working relationships, but little is done to improve working relationships that are operating at 70 percent capacity. For example, what might be the typical reaction when a supervisor intentionally intimidates employees from expressing their opinion by threatening retaliation, or when one manager continues to act in a manner that encourages other managers to work around him or her? (Sometimes people treat each other like babies treat diapers!) Some loud complaints may emerge from the peer group or the direct reports affected, but that is generally the extent of the reaction. Even if the up-line supervisor is aware of the disruption, a typical response sounds something like, "That's just Larry. I've got to talk to him about that sometime." Such episodes of inefficient teamwork when left uncorrected serve to continuously steal money from the financial bottom line.

The asymmetrical emphasis between the technical and people tracks was recently discussed with the vice president of one of our well-known financial services companies who stated that his industry seeks to remove the people element by creating opportunities for the consumer to interact via the Internet to control their financial investments. Though this act of consumer control may reduce the dependency upon company employees, people have to be in the formula. Without people there is no company. The very ideas to create the new opportunities for consumer control originated from the brain of a human being!

The point is that everything begins with people! Even making money.

3. *Why do companies tolerate loss of income attributed to people problems?* Leaders and managers are not held truly accountable to implement the building blocks of teamwork: communication, cooperation, trust, and respect.

Accountability simply means ensuring that people do what is expected to be done within defined timeframes. Accountability sounds simple to implement, but unfortunately, that is not the case. Not holding people accountable for what they have agreed to do is a constant complaint in corporate communities. One could easily conclude that such lackluster performance is accepted as the glue that holds organizations together. Scary thought, isn't it? But you probably can't even begin to count the number of times you've said or heard someone say something that sounds like, "I can't understand why the boss keeps Larry around anyway. He is totally non-cooperative. The only agenda is his agenda. The work flow would be so much smoother if Larry's career were recycled to another organization." Larry's boss loses credibility, and morale suffers as the message goes out through the organization that being uncooperative is okay. Unfortunately, lack of accountability is frequently perceived as an organizational plague that's crippling efficiency.

Failure of accountability was cited as a primary reason that 70 percent of the CEOs fail and are subsequently fired, according to Ram Charan and Geoffrey Colvin, who wrote the article, "Why CEOs Fail," published in *Fortune* magazine (June 21, 1999).

4. *Why are people not held accountable for teamwork?* Fear is a major contributor. First is the fear associated with teaching teamwork or interpersonal skills. The development track for leaders and managers focuses primarily (or entirely) on a career's technical aspects. Training on how to work with people is conspicuously absent from college curricula. A lack of formal knowledge speaks to one reason that people are uncomfortable working with such behaviors.

The situation is exacerbated by the popularity of current terminology that speaks of "soft skills" when referring to interpersonal skills as compared with "hard skills" associated with the technical characteristics of job performance. The bewildering question looming in the minds of most people is, "How do you work with such soft and touchy-feely behaviors?"

Psychologically speaking, "hard" implies greater importance than "soft." Webster defines "hard" in terms of strength and "soft" in terms of being weak, delicate, and not strong, which is not the message we want people to receive, given that people power fuels the engine that drives the train of change, performance, and financial success.

Consequently, we're advocating a change in the accepted terminology to remove the dichotomy of "hard" versus "soft." For that reason, synonymously throughout this book we use concepts like teamwork behaviors, interpersonal behaviors, interpersonal performance, people skills, workplace behaviors, and social behaviors.

Second is the fear associated with the defensive reaction to protect one's ego. An automatic defense system comes into play whenever you are threatened by an element in your environment. Consider what happens in the pit of your own stomach any time someone offers you even the most constructive feedback about improving your performance. Learning what you can do to improve is usually not a pleasant event—even when you know it is the truth! The uncomfortableness is generated by a gap between how you want your actions to be perceived by others and the reality of how these actions are perceived. Most of us become supersensitive; muscles tighten and nervousness takes immediate control of our body. These reactions consist of a cluster of behaviors associated with the natural law of survival. You want to defend yourself, fight back, and set the person straight.

You know all of this because you've experienced it, and you know that many people do not have the self-discipline to effectively manage these ego-driven behaviors. Consequently some individuals participate in a host of defensive behaviors, including outbursts of anger and denial. The discussion can quickly become a shouting match or a standoff between two different opinions. Such behaviors are not easy, nor comfortable to work with, thereby eliciting the natural response to avoid what is uncomfortable. It's just easier not to deal with these people issues, so you let the person(s) in question continue to learn through the trial-and-error method—that is, you let them shoot themselves in the foot. Doing so is certainly not doing anyone a favor, but it's easier and more comfortable that way.

We are reminded of a production manager who had the reputation of being a know-it-all hothead. He was disliked, feared, and avoided. His supervisor was aware of the tip of the iceberg, but never discussed the issue with him. The supervisor preferred to avoid the man rather than cope with his behavior constructively. Finally the situation grew so serious that it led to a confrontation. You can imagine the reaction of the production manager—denial—and in the end his people incompetence derailed his career at this facility.

Third is the uncertainty associated with the abstract nature of such teamwork values as open communication, trust, and respect. People behaviors are unquestionably more abstract and difficult to define than technical skills. This abstraction contributes to confusion and fear.

Consider that every technical task is tangible and has an associated process to be completed. The simple act of putting gasoline in your car has a defined process that can be observed. The presence of a tangible process allows you to teach the process. That is, when you have an employee who lacks the necessary technical knowledge or skill to correctly complete a job task, you can teach the process to improve the performance.

Traditionally, people behaviors have not been considered a tangible process, therefore lacking well-defined performance standards. For example, what are your performance standards for being friendly, openly communicating, or trusting?

Suppose your employees' job responsibilities require friendly interactions with internal and/or external customers. Which behaviors would the employees be expected to use in the workplace to act in a friendly manner? Which behaviors are you to teach and for which are employees to be held accountable? In other words, what is the behavioral process to be friendly?

Interpersonal performance and teamwork have traditionally not been defined in terms of performance standards, which contributed to not holding people accountable.

5. *Why are people afraid?* The presence of fear signals the need for more self-confidence. Self-confidence comes from doing what causes discomfort. As the titular words of the best-selling book by Susan Jeffers, Ph.D., say, *Face the Fear and Do It Anyway.*

Let's begin to answer the question posed in this section by asking, "Do you experience fear when completing job responsibilities that are based on standard operating procedures?" No, because that's just the way the job is done, and you have the necessary self-confidence to complete the procedures.

A primary root cause that creates fear when working with interpersonal skills and teamwork is the lack of standard operating procedures or a systematic manner for carrying out interpersonal job responsibilities. Without standard operating procedures guiding teamwork behaviors or a systematic process for improving working relationships, becoming comfortable with effective workplace interpersonal skills is left to chance and to the whim of each individual's learning curve.

Another complicating factor is who handles the fix and how it is accomplished. Let's contrast humans and machines for just a moment. What happens when you experience a problem with a machine? You may be able to complete minor repairs by following instructions outlined in the service manual. If not, then a well-trained technician fixes it. The technician follows a set of standard operating procedures to diagnose the problem, consider the repair alternatives, implement the best one, and test the repair.

Admittedly, working with people is more difficult than working with machines. To begin with, there is no manual, nor is there a cut-and-dried standard operating procedure. Sometimes the problem is difficult to understand, or even when you understand the problem, knowing what to do presents another challenge. It would be nice to simply dismantle a person's head as if he or she were a machine and tighten a few nuts to adjust that person's thinking, but life isn't that easy. Of course, one alternative is to call Human Resources and send them the problem!

Removing the fear factor is the key to unlocking the door that allows effective teamwork to walk through. Thus, the overall objective of this book is to show you a systems approach for working with teamwork interpersonal behaviors that is based on standard operating procedures. Reliance on a system builds the necessary self-confidence that is the antidote to fear.

The Traditional Method Tried, but Not True

The traditional method to improve teamwork entails defining a teamwork template that looks something like this:

- Ensure the team understands its purpose in the organization.
- Ensure the presence of well-defined common goals that are understood by all team members.
- Define the roles and responsibilities of each team member.

- Establish an accountability procedure to ensure completion of the team's tasks.

This template is obviously important, but by itself, it cannot ensure the work unit's success. For example, a sales staff recently met with its new sales manager. In spite of the department's financial success, the new manager listened to such stinging criticisms as:

- "We are kept in the dark like mushrooms. We don't know what is going on."
- "Whenever we are told what Corporate is going to do, we also know that will never happen."
- "The previous sales manager only contacted us when he wanted to pound on us for not doing our job. We never heard positive words come from his mouth."

You can see where this story is going. Efficient teamwork is more than knowing goals and responsibilities. Efficient teamwork is about working together. The staff asked the new sales manager to keep them informed with the information needed to complete their job responsibilities, fulfill the sales manager's expectations, and follow-through on commitments. Last, but certainly not least, they would like to know when they are doing a good job.

In Closing

It is time to undo the paradox and make teamwork work. Before we put the work in teamwork to work, however, we must have a very serious discussion.

3 | Are You Ready to Put the Work in Teamwork to Work?

In the words of the best-selling author Daniel Goleman, author of *Working with Emotional Intelligence:*

> We now have tons of data documenting the links between emotional intelligence of leaders and performance of the organization. We find a strong and very positive correlation. The more the leader exhibits competencies like initiative, nurture of others, team leadership, self-confidence, drive to achieve, and empathy, the more positive the climate. And the more the organization has that climate, the better its business performance as measured by profit growth, net operating income, growth in sales, return on sales, growth in earnings and attaining business goals.

Setting a Good Example Is One of Your More Challenging Assignments

The question before you now is what behaviors do you want integrated into your teamwork culture? Do you create a workplace like that described by Goleman and harness the

19

frustration in working relationships to use it to improve individual performance and associated working relationships, or do you allow it to act like an undetected computer virus, cutting away at the morale, production, and consequently profits?

The adverse impact of workplace frustration reminds us about a news story heard on National Public Radio concerning a new strain of termites that is invading the historical structures in New Orleans, Louisiana. This ferocious strain is devastating and usually is undetected until the inside of the wood is eaten away and the structure collapses. Unbridled frustration can have a similar devastating effect upon an organization. Most of the listeners to the termite story are not directly affected by those ferocious wood-eating creatures and thereby are concerned and feel sorry for those who are adversely impacted, but they remain somewhat detached while hoping something is discovered to control their spread into unaffected geographies or to eradicate those critters. Similarly, individuals hear about the horror and war stories within other companies and remain somewhat detached while being concerned and empathetic. But they are directly impacted by the lack of teamwork within their organization and want the problem eradicated—either by improving working relationships with the existing team members or recycling to another organization those who do not want to be team players.

Are You Ready to Maximize Frustration?

As you ponder the dilemma of whether to take advantage of this opportunity or not, some very important questions can be taken into consideration, and the answers to those questions can help you decide a direction for you and your organization. The overriding question is, "Do you want to implement a systematic process to maximize the development of your people—your most valuable asset—or is the present status quo okay?"

Each of the following questions is designed to encourage you to think about your willingness to take the lead in establishing a corporate culture committed to improving the teamwork and interpersonal skills throughout your organization. The diagnostic nature of each question speaks to an integral leadership characteristic required to successfully implement the systematic process detailed in this book. Please take a few minutes to consider each question.

	Yes	No
1. Are you willing to participate in a process to continuously develop your own social skills?	—	—
2. Are you willing to lead by example, even if that means changing yourself even more than those with whom you work may change?	—	—
3. Are you ready to devote the resources necessary to change your teamwork culture?	—	—
4. Are you willing to be held accountable and measure your own success by the same standards that will apply to others?	—	—
5. Are you willing to hold other staff accountable to implement the change process?	—	—

We understand that you may seem a bit uncomfortable answering these questions without knowing more about what the subsequent chapters present. Your answers, though, are crucial to the commitment that leaders must make to successfully implement the processes we discuss in detail. At this point, suffice it to say that top-down change is the only way to produce bottom-up commitment throughout your organization.

In Closing

If your answer to any of the listed questions is no, then you need to ask yourself whether you are serious about developing a process to improve the people side of your organization. If not, we would encourage you to read this book out of curiosity, but refrain from implementing the process. The last thing we want to do is to contribute another entrant into your organization's idea-of-the-month cemetery.

We do, however, want to contribute to the vitality and the health of the people in your organization and to its overall success. So we hope you answered each question yes, and that you continue reading with the full intention of putting these words into action.

Part Two
PEOPLE SYSTEMS

4 | Entering the People Age

A characteristic common to your company and a train is the fact that both require two tracks to be successful. Visualize the two iron rails of the railroad track going into the distant future. Suppose one is maintained well while the other one is allowed to enter a state of disrepair. The eventual fate is a derailed train.

Consider the two tracks of your company. One is the technical track: doing what the company is in the business of doing. The second is the people track. Think of these two tracks running parallel, like railroad tracks. What will be your company's fate if both tracks are not well maintained?

Traditionally, which of these two tracks receives the most attention? The typical answer is the technical track. Before we address the logical reasons underpinning the asymmetrical emphasis favoring the technical track, let's take a closer look at the operating elements commonly implemented in corporate communities to promote their growth and continued success. As you review the list in the following table, note which of these exist in your company and whether they apply to the technical or the people track.

OPERATING ELEMENTS

Systems

Company vision statement	Technical / People
Company mission statement	Technical / People
Strategic plan	Technical / People
Job descriptions and performance evaluations	Technical / People
Employee training	Technical / People
Quality management/ continuous improvement	Technical / People
Preventive maintenance	Technical / People
Performance measurement systems	Technical / People

Keeping in mind that successful people create successful organizations, let's briefly examine each of these elements.

1. Company Vision Statement

Can you imagine a company functioning without a vision driving its future? That would be like blindfolding a great marksman, turning him/her around several times, and expecting the bullet to hit the bull's-eye.

To put it another way, an organization is a living entity and, like every living entity, is in the process of creating and becoming. Without a vision to guide its growth, a company may find itself involved in a multitude of activities that reach out in seemingly random directions, like the tentacles of an octopus. Some of these activities may not promote organizational health.

James Collins and Jerry Porras, in their best-selling book *Built to Last: Successful Habits of Visionary Companies,* chronicle how successful companies defined and used their vision to guide their companies to profitability and higher levels of achievement and success.

A Vision for Developing People Assets

People are generally mentioned in the traditional vision statements, but consider a statement focusing on the vision to develop people assets of the company and the determinants of the company's growth and success—its people and how people work together. This statement would define the values and behaviors to be institutionalized within your company's belief system and behavioral repertoire. We're not talking about another decoration for the wall, but a working statement that is institutionalized as an integral component of your culture and measured to hold people accountable for the statement's implementation.

2. Company Mission Statement

At one point or another in the recent past, most organizations followed the movement to develop mission statements describing the purpose of the organization. Unfortunately the mission statement movement has degenerated into a fad, because after writing these nice-sounding words, the statement was proudly placed on the wall beside the vision statement, in the company's official publications, and then soon forgotten. It's a shame when such a useful tool is allowed to atrophy.

Testimony to its lack of use is offered by the seminar participants we've asked to volunteer to quote their company's mission statement, but only a few brave souls have attempted that feat. Once, while working with a group of state highway patrolmen, a volunteer came forward and described his organization's mission statement in vague statements. Later he admitted being a member of the team that had written it. Upon seeing him several months later, he mentioned being so embarrassed about not being able to quote something he had helped to write that he'd since committed it to memory.

The People Mission

Like the vision statement, the mission statement usually mentions the importance of employees. We're advocates for writing and using a statement speaking to the issue to maximize the potential of every employee and the three working relationships that determine the financial success of the company.

1. Among members of the work unit.
2. Between work units.
3. Between employees and their leader.

The people mission focuses on employees working together to help each other to be more successful.

3. Strategic Plans

An organization must also know how its vision will be achieved, theoretically through a carefully written strategic plan. Strategic plans are usually translated into departmental goals and objectives, accompanied by some means of measurement to provide accountability and feedback regarding the progress made toward achieving these objectives. A strategic plan is a useful tool to align the resources and energies of an organization to create the necessary synergy for the growth of the business.

People's Strategic Plan

A strategic plan to improve teamwork or an individual's interpersonal effectiveness can also be defined, implemented, and measured. That plan can speak to what must be done for employees to integrate such behavioral values as trust, cooperation, respect, and communication, to name a few, into the workplace environment.

Consider the fact that you are a small business unit selling your knowledge and skills to your company. A primary difference between the company and each individual employee is that the company is selling its products or services to many customers, whereas you are selling to only one customer—the company itself. The strategies designed to improve your interpersonal effectiveness and create synergy in working relationships can help make you too valuable to lose.

4. Job Descriptions

Oh yes, the infamous job description. Many organizations have them, or at least some minimal documentation of what is expected from each employee. There are a variety of ways to write a job description, and how to do so is not the subject of this book. We do want to point out that such descriptions traditionally speak to completing the technical requirements of the job and only rarely include a list of the expected people behaviors that drive high performance.

People Job Description

The natural extension is to apply the interpersonal behaviors the employee is expected to exhibit to improving both their interpersonal performance and working relationships. Upon adding the expected people behaviors, the job description can serve as the comprehensive communication tool to outline the behaviors expected for successful performance.

5. Training

In this era of rapid technological change, employees must be continually trained in the new technologies and methods if the company wants to remain on the cutting edge of competition in their market segment.

Training on People Skills

Training to improve interpersonal effectiveness and working relationships is another matter. Traditionally it's a hit-or-miss process—if it's done at all. Two CEOs attending a seminar were overheard to state that they had each put training on customer service issues "on the back burner because there were just too many other alligators to fight." Now here's the kicker: one of these top managers represented a financial institution, the other headed a medical center. Can you think of any industries where customer service is in as much demand as a bank and a medical center in today's marketplace, and these CEOs said customer service is not important? Can you imagine the consequences when the CEOs feel as though they haven't the time to improve their service to customers?

The bottom line is that training on interpersonal behaviors needs to support the values and behaviors being institutionalized by the organization to improve the working relationships. And just as important is the need for a comprehensive systematic process to measure the transfer of learning and hold people accountable to implement the behaviors taught in the classroom.

6. Continuous Improvement

The era of quality management, with its intent to capitalize on employee input, emerged from the need for U.S. companies to compete with foreign producers of goods and services. No one can argue with the intent of the quality movement to create a satisfied customer with improved service levels and quality products. Sadly, this movement has received a black eye in some corporate communities, because considerable financial resources were focused on this effort without yielding a significant financial return. The blame has often been laid at the feet of the quality tools rather than at the people who use these tools. We must remember that people serve as the gateways to organizational change. Even though your company may not have a formal quality improvement process, common sense dictates that you must be on the edge of the comfort zone to continually improve your product/service and customer service to remain competitive and succeed.

People Continuous Improvement

Speaking of commonsense management also dictates that we apply the concept of continuous improvement to the people processes. There is only one way to achieve that objective: the guiding behavioral values and their respective definitions need to be defined. Once defined, their implementation must be measured to continuously monitor the working relationships. In doing so, strengths and weaknesses can be quantified to provide the opportunity to pinpoint the areas needing improvement in an effort to maximize return on this effort.

7. Preventive Maintenance

There is no doubt about the benefit of a preventive maintenance program to maximize equipment efficiency leading to an ongoing revenue stream. When the machine is responsible for producing thousands of dollars of product each and every day, a major effort is needed to keep those machines operating at 100 percent efficiency.

People Preventive Maintenance Systems

We need a parallel process for people maintenance. First, the company needs to identify, measure, and monitor key people behaviors that drive the success of working relationships. Second is the need to create the corporate mindset to identify and fix any frustration in working relationships that could lead to a people failure which interrupts the revenue stream. This corporate mentality is in sharp contrast to the often-used approach to "see no evil, hear no evil, speak no evil," and it will go away.

8. Measurements

Can you imagine an organization operating without data? It's almost absurd to think about, let alone write about, but visualize an organization without data:

- There would be no way to know the financial status.
- You would not know if the manufacturing or production processes were occurring.
- The quality of the product or service delivered would not be known.
- Maintenance would not be an issue, as you would never know when equipment needed maintenance.

Enough of this absurdity. An organization without data is analogous to a human body without a nervous system. You would not know if you were hungry or thirsty, and if you ever started to eat or drink, you would eat or drink yourself to death as you would not know when to stop. You may never go to bed, but if you did, you might not wake up. Then, of course, without data you would be forever lost, for you would not know where you are.

We could continue, but we're certain you see the point. Data tell you where you are, which is a requirement in order for you to go where you want to be.

People Measurements

Traditionally considerable asymmetry exists between the sophistication of the approach to obtaining production numbers and people numbers. The typical data used to gauge people behaviors is a short list.

- Employee turnover
- Absenteeism
- Tardiness
- Use of sick leave and other measures
- Grievances/unfair labor complaints
- EEOC complaints

None of these focus on the process of developing people. They are simply indicators of organizational issues such as employee morale and people management.

In all fairness, in case we sound too harsh, many organizations have implemented employee development and measuring systems that include the following.

- Records detailing the participation in training programs.
- Annual employee satisfaction or climate surveys.
- 360° multi-rater environments.

The first one is a record-keeping function. The second one often produces a great-looking report that is frequently put on the shelf. The 360° multi-rater environment can be a powerful tool when used correctly, but unfortunately unless used carefully it will be placed in the same category as total quality management and other organizational dinosaurs. We've seen too many instances in which:

- Those who received the feedback were left to figure out what they can do to improve the scores.
- Specific action plans were not developed subsequent to a 360° assessment process.
- The immediate supervisors of those receiving 360° feedback did not follow up with the employee.

That such valuable resources are wasted is a shame. The same organizational disease that tried to kill the total quality management movement appears to be attacking the multi-rater assessment environment; the immunity system of the existing organization's culture is killing these foreign substances entering into its comfort zone.

Emphasis on Technical vs. People Performance

Logical reasons exist for the asymmetrical attention given to the technical track of an organization compared to the people track, and we must meet the challenge that each presents.

The technical track has been perceived as the profit generator. If you were asked why your company exists, the logical answer would be to generate profits for the stakeholders. If you were asked the follow-up question of how your company generates profits, the logical answer would be through selling products or services. Who makes the products and delivers the services that generate profits? The obvious answer: People do. Without people, there is no product, service, or profit, as those elements are the by-products of people working together. In reality, people working together are the profit generators.

The people track is more abstract. One of the focuses of this book is to make abstract social skills more empirical. Consider the fact that successfully completing technical responsibilities requires adhering to well-defined processes. Because these processes are empirical, they can be readily taught, repeated, and measured.

The abstract nature of social skills presents the interesting challenge of making them more empirical so they can be readily taught, repeated, and measured. For example, you want your employees to be friendly to each other and to your customers, right? What empirical process must your employees use to demonstrate friendliness? What is friendliness? What does friendliness look like? How can you teach it? Can friendliness be measured?

To be taught, repeated, and measured, this abstract social skill must be defined by observable behaviors. In other words, the definition creates a process that employees can follow to create friendliness. This process may include the following behaviors:

1. Offer a smile.
2. Use a friendly greeting, for example, "Thank you for shopping with us."
3. Use the other person's name whenever possible.
4. Talk in terms of the other person's interest.
5. Use your sense of humor to laugh at yourself and funny situations. As a sidebar, laughter is the quickest way

to connect with another person.

Defining this process helps make abstract social skills empirical, which is essential to institutionalizing the behavior into your culture. Defining abstract social skills as specific behavioral processes allows them to be taught, repeated, and measured, and you will learn more about this process in chapter 5.

Afraid to work with people issues. To begin with, employees are not taught to work with the people track as they are the technical track, for the obvious reason that gainful employment is dependent upon successfully completing one's technical responsibilities. You don't want an employee who can't meet the quality and safety standards associated with their technical job responsibilities, so the training emphasis for both the employee and the supervisor has been to complete these responsibilities successfully. Another reason training on working with people issues is not readily provided is the reputation that such training does not produce a return on its financial investment. In other words, training on interpersonal performance and people skills has the reputation of not working! Admittedly, challenges must be met to ensure such training does work, and those are discussed in chapter 15.

To complicate matters, dealing with people issues engages the ego. That is, even constructive criticism designed to improve the employee's performance can be met with a barrage of defensiveness. Such resistance is typically uncomfortable, and given that the body is constructed to avoid pain while seeking pleasure, the natural tendency is to avoid those situations that are deemed uncomfortable. Consequently, the acceptable margin of error is much greater for the successful completion of interpersonal competencies than for technical competencies. In some instances, interpersonal incompetence is ignored in favor of technical competence.

The bottom line is that many employees (including supervisors) don't know how to work with people issues because the learning track to work with such people has been by trial and error rather than classroom instruction. This lack of knowledge compounds the degree of fear or uncomfortableness to work with people issues, so they go unattended.

The measurement challenge. Computer programs generate numbers associated with technical performance, and in some instances, more reports than can be used in an effort to maximize performance and profitability. Monitoring technical performance has a decided advantage over using numbers to monitor the use of interpersonal behaviors. For the moment we need only to acknowledge that interpersonal performance driving teamwork can be measured and monitored. We defer further discussion of the challenges of doing so to our more detailed presentation in chapter 8.

In Closing

We can do better. It is time to do better.

It's time to enter the people age and use a systems approach to improve people performance in a manner similar to technical improvements. The organization's most important asset is no longer going to be left to the whim of personalities and a random, haphazard development process. The systems approach to implement the people operating systems includes the following four components.

1. A TeamWork Values Statement to define the desired teamwork culture that guides the development.

2. A measurement system to identify strengths and weaknesses in the three components of the people operating system: the working relationships among members of the work unit, between employees and their supervisor, and between work units. To simplify the process, we've developed the MBC Software® (*M*easuring *B*ehavior *C*hange) methodologies so employees can easily, quickly, and confidentially measure the use of the desired behaviors in the workplace environment. Use of the MBC Software® provides measurements

and feedback in real time, which are essential both to managing the people operating systems and to holding the improvement process accountable.

3. Defining and measuring the impact of behavioral strategies to improve the working relationship.

4. Ongoing measurements to monitor the organization's health that parallels those employed on the technical track, allowing you to minimize frustrations in working relationships that interfere with generating profits.

5 | The TeamWork Values Statement

"To get to your destination, you must know where you want to go." A simple and trite statement, but true.

Can you imagine the confusion, chaos, and emotional outbursts that would take place if the destination point for your family vacation was not final on the morning you were to depart? You could wander around, like unlucky tourists driving lost in a strange city, but is that a wise use of your time and other resources? Is that the way you want to live your life? Develop your career? Develop your business?

The principle of knowing where you want to go is the foundation of sound business practices. Numerous authors, consultants, and speakers have long emphasized the importance of creating a vision statement to guide companies into their future.

We've already referenced the best-selling book *Built to Last: Successful Habits of Visionary Companies*, by James Collins and Jerry Porras. These authors describe the characteristics of highly successful companies such as Walt Disney, Wal-Mart, Nordstrom, 3M, Ford Motor Company, and Hewlett-Packard. The common denominator is that each is consistently implementing a vision and a set of values that drive the success of the company. Now we are going to unleash the power of a vision to develop people and their working relationships.

Writing a TeamWork Values Statement

The first step is knowing where you want to go, which means writing a TeamWork Values Statement to define the teamwork values and specific behaviors to drive the success of your people operating systems.

Mentioning writing a TeamWork Values Statement frequently elicits eye-rolling gestures, as if to say, "Oh no, not this process again." But the TeamWork Values Statement is a working statement that defines how employees in the organization are expected to work together. The base statement is no longer than twenty-five words to direct the participants to identify the most important behavioral values and facilitate ease of remembering and applying the final product.

The statement is used throughout the organization, so the first step is to obtain input from employees throughout the organization. Our typical procedure is to use several groups of employees, mixing management staff within each group, and to give each the same mission: describe the ideal workplace environment in terms of human behaviors. The final document emerges from the input offered by the participants.

Scheduling employee involvement has several advantages.

- An immediate message is sent throughout the organization about the importance of workplace relationships.
- Everyone's ownership of and commitment to the effort increases.
- Diversity leads to more innovative insights and ideas.

- The final statement is more representative of the organization.

Let's look at a few examples from real organizations:

Realizing each individual is a vital link in our organization, we honestly communicate; exhibit patience, respect, and trust; acknowledge a job well done; and cooperate toward our common goal.

ABC Company's employees are committed professionals creating a teamwork environment established on the principles of respect, communication, trust, and fairness.

The ABC plant is a learning organization characterized by professionalism, open communication, teamwork, respect, and trust, and at all times acting with integrity to create positive, high-performing teams.

Defining Teamwork Behaviors

If knowing where you want to go is the first step, the second is knowing how to get there.

People practice this principle every day. For example, every job function has an established procedure for a successful completion. If a new employee does not have either the required job knowledge or skills to satisfactorily complete the technical requirements of the job, the individual receives additional training.

Those rather abstract TeamWork Values need to be addressed in exactly the same manner. A behavioral process needs to be defined so that the skill can be repeated and taught in a manner similar to the technical responsibilities of any job.

Let's use the corporate scapegoat, open communication, as an example. When you talk about communication, what exactly are you referring to? What process do you use to ensure that effective communication occurs? If you were my mentor within an organization and were going to teach me to communicate effectively, what would you teach me to do?

The first response we receive upon asking such questions is usually a blank stare, followed by "I don't know." Communication is not traditionally thought of as a process. It's just another one of those abstract words we use to describe some phenomenon that involves a sender and a receiver. People might not have been able to define it, but they know for certain that it creates havoc and causes major problems within organizations. A procedure that can begin the creative flow of ideas is to ask employees to complete the sentence, "We know we are communicating when we . . ." Employees typically define communication to include a combination of the following behaviors:

- Encourage the expression of ideas and opinions.
- Allow freedom to express opinions (without fear of reprisal).
- Present the facts of the situation.
- Keep people informed.
- Offer to those affected by the decision the opportunity to provide input into that decision.
- Admit making a mistake.
- Admit having limited knowledge.

Behavioral definitions specify the behaviors that can be seen and then taught, institutionalized, and quantified to pinpoint specific behaviors that contribute to success as well as interruptions in the communication process.

The behavioral definitions that are typically included for three other behavioral values common to most organizations are as follows:

Respect

- Ask others for their input.
- Listen to understand that input.
- Use that input whenever possible.
- Give credit where credit is due (recognize jobs well done).
- Explain, if applicable, why certain input could not be used.
- Allow people to do their jobs.
- Accept your coworkers as individuals.

Trust

- Be dependable by doing what you say you will do.
- Empower people with the authority to do their jobs.
- Keep confidential information confidential.
- Keep people informed with the facts.

Cooperation/Teamwork

- Understand what others need from you.
- Assist others to meet the defined needs with a sense of urgency.
- Volunteer to assist others as needed.
- Provide others feedback about meeting the defined needs.

- Willingly accept feedback provided by others about meeting the defined needs.
- Base decisions on a win/win philosophy.

Examples of Completed TeamWork Values Statements

We are including two examples to illustrate the final document. The first is being used within a healthcare environment and the second within a manufacturing facility.

In the twenty-first century, ABC Company self-directed teams consist of colleagues who have a shared sense of purpose, support each other, openly communicate, and are innovative, trustworthy, respectful, and accountable.

Self-directed

- We empower team members to make decisions closer to the customer.
- We use our authority to go the extra mile to meet each other's needs.
- We competently use our authority.
- We make decisions through consensus.

Shared sense of purpose

- We work to meet ABC Company's Vision, Mission, Guiding Principles, and Core Goals.
- We define our common goals.

- We understand our common goals.
- We are held accountable to achieve our common goals.

Support each other

- We understand what we need from each other.
- We proactively meet the needs of others to help each other to be successful.
- We recognize each other for a job well done.

Openly communicate

- We present the facts of the situation.
- We feel free to express our ideas.
- We objectively accept diverse ideas.
- We openly discuss the behaviors to be implemented to improve teamwork.

Innovative

- We encourage the expression of new ideas.
- We willingly try new ideas.
- We practice the philosophy, "Mistakes are learning opportunities for competence building."

Trustworthy

- We are dependable and do what we agree to do.
- We keep confidential information confidential.
- We keep each other informed with the necessary information.
- We are consistent so team members know what to expect from each other.

Respectful

- We accept our individual differences.
- We listen to understand the input offered by others.

- We use other's input whenever possible.
- We tell each other how their input was used.

Accountable

- We competently complete our job responsibilities.
- We competently complete our responsibilities in support of the team's decisions.
- We provide each other feedback regarding the progress of meeting each other's needs.
- We accept the feedback offered to improve performance.
- We do what needs to be done to implement the Team-Work Values Statement.

The second example is:

ABC Company's employees are committed professionals creating a teamwork environment built on the principles of respect, communication, trust, and being fair.

Committed

- We do whatever is necessary to competently complete our job responsibilities.
- We volunteer to assist each other whenever possible.

Professionals

- We remain emotionally calm when working with each other.
- We are engaged in the process of continuous learning to improve our personal performance.

- We look for the good in every situation.
- We use mistakes as learning opportunities.

Teamwork

- We understand what we need from each other.
- We work to meet each other's needs with a sense of urgency.
- We provide each other feedback regarding the quality of work and meeting the defined needs.
- We willingly accept feedback about meeting each other's needs in an effort to ensure the success of our internal customer.
- We recognize each other for a job well done.
- We make team decisions.
- We support our team's decisions.

Respect

- We ask each other for input.
- We listen to understand the input or point of view offered by others.
- We use that input whenever possible.
- We provide an explanation as to why the input offered by others was not used.
- We accept each other as individuals.

Communication

- We structure input from others into decisions that affect them.
- We feel free to express our ideas.
- We keep each other informed with the facts of the situation.
- We admit our mistakes.
- We admit when we don't have the necessary information.

- We agree to disagree to use diverse ideas to make better decisions.

Trust

- We empower by ensuring that people have the necessary authority to do their jobs.
- We exhibit dependability by doing what we agree to do.
- We keep confidential information confidential.

Being fair

- We apply policies and procedures consistently.
- We make decisions based on facts.

Benefits Associated with Implementing a TeamWork Values Statement

Defines the direction for the future. The TeamWork Values Statement and its behavioral definitions provide a clear direction for the future and a behavioral road map to get you to where you want to go.

Everyone knows the expected behaviors. James Collins and Jerry Porras, in their book *Built to Last: Successful Habits of Visionary Companies,* use the expression "cult-like behaviors" to describe the process of institutionalizing core values. These authors cited examples like Sam Walton's famous rule that "anytime an Associate was within ten feet of a customer, s/he was expected to smile and use a friendly greeting" and Nordstrom's motto, "Service to the customer above all else!"

The TeamWork Values Statement presents the desired values and the cultlike behaviors that need to be institutionalized to ensure that the behaviors associated with each respective value walk the corporate hallways. The statement serves as a formal description of the desired culture independently of personalities. Without such a statement the behaviors used to work with each other are left to the discretion of the individuals' personalities. That scary thought becomes even scarier as you consider the variety of personalities that compose your management team. In other words, each manager is writing his or her own culture so the resulting culture is a mixture of personalities rather than a disciplined approach to ensure that everyone is using the same interpersonal behaviors or standard operating procedures to create the desired teamwork culture. It's no wonder that teamwork is often a mess!

Most organizations have well-defined systems to ensure high performance of every major technical component of the business. The major void is not having a system to guide high interpersonal performance and working relationships within the people operating system, in spite of the organizational truism that people drive the success of the company. The TeamWork Values Statement is the first step to complete that void.

Job description. Think of these blueprint definitions as a behavioral job description. All managers and team leaders must absolutely walk the talk of the words included within this statement. For that reason, we caution managers to ensure that every definition included in the statement is in fact a behavior that will be institutionalized, behaviors that they themselves will manifest. Nothing is more disheartening than to create the expectation that something will happen when it does not, or to espouse a value and behavior that the organization's leaders fail to adopt themselves.

We're putting the cart before the horse a little, but because managers lead by example, they are encouraged to read this TeamWork Values Statement daily as a reminder of how they are expected to behave during the course of the day. In later chapters, you learn about a process to measure the use of these behaviors. In fact, we often hear people comment that the act of measuring the implementation of these behaviors serves to remind them of the importance of modeling them.

Teaching a behavioral process. These behavioral definitions provide the opportunity to teach a process to implement the respective social skill. Think about the positive ramifications of these definitions. First, you have a defined process, a standard operating procedure, performance standards, or whatever term you want to use to reflect the existence of these behaviors, just as you have processes to complete the technical requirements of your job. Second, because the behaviors are tangible, you can easily teach others the processes for communication, demonstrating trust, respect, or whatever teamwork social skill you wish to see reflected within your corporate culture.

Our contention is that you already know how to implement these behaviors and that you even use them from time to time. The real issue is converting these words into action—that is, consistently doing what you already know. The organizational challenge is to structure a performance management system to institutionalize the cultlike behaviors that already exist in your behavioral library.

Measurement. The tangible behavioral definitions allow their use to be measured and the data employed to improve performance as is done with technical processes. You learn in the next chapter about a comprehensive measurement system to quantify the use of the behaviors contained in the TeamWork Values Statement.

Psychological message. The process of defining and implementing the TeamWork Values Statement sends a powerful message to all employees about the importance of teamwork. It demonstrates to present and future employees that your company cares about maximizing its number-one asset: its people.

Consider two companies. One we'll call the "I Don't Care" Company and the second the "I Care" Company. Suppose the "I Don't Care" Company could be described by such behaviors as:

- When we want your opinion we'll ask for it; until then, keep your nose to the grindstone.
- We pay you to do a job, not to talk.
- Empowerment means "we'll do it my way, until I tell you differently."
- Teamwork means you help me, and I'll help you when I get the time.

Contrast these behaviors with the "I Care" Company, which has written and is integrating their TeamWork Values Statement into their day-to-day operations. With which of the two companies would you rather work? Ample evidence in today's business world supports the fact that being an "I Care" type of company leads to higher morale, productivity, and creativity. It positions the company to employ and retain valuable employees. All of these factors are important contributors to growing a successful and profitable company.

In Closing

Knowing where you want to go and how to get there are the crucial first steps in the process to improve your teamwork culture. The next challenge is putting the words contained in your TeamWork Values Statement to work for you.

6 | Using People Operating Systems to Enter the People Age

Let's begin this chapter with a bit of humor. Imagine what your organization would be like if . . .

- Every department were allowed to create its own financial systems.
- Every department were allowed to create its own human resources policies and procedures.
- Every production unit were allowed to establish its own operating systems.
- Every department were allowed to implement its own quality standards.

The end result might not be so humorous. The chaos and confusion would be extremely uncomfortable and could lead to the company's demise. That is not the future you are working to achieve, so operating systems and procedures are implemented to ensure order and your company's success.

Similarly the end result in the absence of a systems approach for working relationships is not a humorous one. As a matter of fact, it's astonishing how we fail to work with each other. It's also amazing how these frustrations are allowed to remain unattended and even perpetuated. Yet that's exactly what happens, as the following examples so clearly illustrate.

A case in point occurred at thirty thousand feet. Several team members, we'll call them Team A, were flying to a meeting with Team B at a sister location. Team A was responsible for producing two parts that were used by Team B. One of the employees from Team A told his team leader that Team B planned to ask Team A to put a differentiating mark on the two parts. As it stood then, both parts looked identical and each had to be installed before knowing if it was the correct part. Obviously, a waste of man-hours occurred when the incorrect part was installed as it had to be removed and another installed until they got the right one. Upon hearing this request, the team leader for Team A made the teamwork statement of the day when he said, "That is a ridiculous request. If they wanted us to mark the parts, they should have asked us to do that before we started production. We're not going to start now!" An excellent opportunity was wasted to use frustration in the workplace as an opportunity to improve working relationships. The manager got an "F" on his teamwork report card.

Consider a manufacturing facility with a history of showing a lack of cooperation between maintenance and production (sound familiar?). Finger pointing is the rule rather than the exception. Employees described the scene as one of complete chaos as managers protected their turf while covering their mistakes. The hourly employees exclaimed that if the managers would just leave them alone, the maintenance and production employees could easily work together. Empowerment, though, is not a tool often used by turf warriors.

The perceived need to remain quiet and protect oneself raised its ugly head and prevented effective teamwork between two departments in yet another organization. While working with teamwork issues, an observation was made to senior managers about the lack of cooperation and trust between two departments. Members of Department A often had to visually inspect the work of Department B. Each episode costs several hundred dollars in wasted time. Upon hearing the observation, one of the senior managers immediately became defensive and exclaimed that the observation was inaccurate. He admitted the problem once existed, but it had been fixed two years ago. Guess what? The problem had not been fixed, and the waste of staff time continued to be the rule rather than the exception. Down-line staff were afraid to inform the senior managers about the nature and extent of the problem because they feared reprisal; messengers were often sacrificed in that organization. Perhaps the teamwork principle, "We're guilty until we prove our innocence," would work more efficiently than becoming defensive and blaming.

Examples showing the lack of teamwork are so prevalent that you may have thought we were visiting your workplace as you were reading these examples. The bottom line is that the loss of human potential as well as the financial losses should alarm all of us.

The time has come to end the outrageous behaviors these examples illustrate and put the words in your TeamWork Values Statement to work. Fortunately there is a better way to conduct business than to allow frustration to run rampant throughout the organization.

A People Operating System

Organizational leaders use two broad principles to guide the technical success of a company. The first is the use of operating systems designed to create an orderly environment to produce the desired end result. Second is the reliance on their systems to pump out data associated with carefully defined performance indicators to know the precise as-is situation on a regular predetermined basis or as needed. As you know, the data these systems provide allow leaders to make necessary adjustments to reach or exceed performance goals and objectives.

We're going to apply this same logic to the three basic working relationships that operate within your company to drive its financial success. These three working relationships compose your "people operating system." These working relationships are

1. Among members of the work unit (including the supervisor/leader).

2. Between work units.

3. Between employees and their supervisor/work unit leader.

Yes, you may have other working relationships—for example, cross-functional teams—but the basic teamwork structure for most organizations comprise these three working relationships.

As you read the following systems approach that underlies the people operating systems, note that the steps are patterned after the systems used to improve the technical performance of your organization. That is, there are two parallel systems. One is used to monitor and improve technical performance, and the second is used to monitor and improve interpersonal performance within the people operating system.

- Chapter 5 introduced the concept of the TeamWork Values Statement to provide the behavioral template for the organization. The behaviors contained in this statement detail the behavioral process to institutionalize the values. In other words, these behaviors constitute a behavioral blueprint of performance standards or cultlike behaviors to guide day-to-day working relationships. These behaviors constitute the orderly process to create the desired result described in the TeamWork Values Statement.

- The data that are used to define the as-is situation are generated by employees rating the use of the behaviors or performance standards specified in the TeamWork Values Statement within the people operating system. That is, at a defined time the work unit members log onto the MBC Software® and quantify the extent to which each behavior is being used. Note the slight disparity represented in the data generation between the technical and people operating systems. You have the luxury of using machines to spontaneously generate technical data versus the need for people to generate the data reflecting interpersonal performance. For that reason, chapter 8 addresses the issues associated with using people as the data generators.

- Behavioral strengths and opportunities for improvement are quickly identified through the data, just as the technical data point out the systems that are working efficiently and those that need adjustment to improve performance.

- Just as members of the work unit define intervention strategies to improve technical performance as needed, the raters define behavioral intervention strategies or solutions designed to improve performance within the people operating system as needed. Once defined, these strategies are entered into the software and the raters quantify the degree to which these solutions improve performance, just as measurements are used to determine the success of technical fixes.

- Technical measurements are compiled and reviewed on a regularly scheduled basis, and numbers generated for the people operating systems are reviewed on a regular basis to monitor the ongoing organizational health.

- The technical numbers used to gauge organizational health are available to those managers and employees who need the data. In a similar manner, the data from the people operating systems are likewise available to whoever needs the data to monitor the organizational health. Usually, up-line supervisors have access to their down-line data. The leader who has the responsibility for a given location has access to all data, both technical and those from the people operating systems.

For the purpose of this immediate discussion, additional features of the methodologies to measure interpersonal performance in the people operating system that need to be mentioned are as follows:

- Individuals can enter data in a manner of minutes.
- The data are confidential.
- The ease of data entry allows the opportunity to obtain measurements on a regularly defined timeline.
- The data are available in real time.
- Data can be generated as frequently as needed.

Putting the TeamWork Values Statement to Work

To illustrate the application of a performance system to maximize the efficiency of the people operating system, let's use a fictional company we'll call The Cole Company. Although the names of individuals are likewise fictitious, the examples used to illustrate the process are based on real-life instances.

The employees at The Cole Company wrote the following TeamWork Values Statement:

Cole Company consists of empowered, innovative professionals who exhibit teamwork based on open communication, trust, respect, and accountability.

Empowered colleagues

- We empower team members to make decisions closer to the customer.

- We use our authority to go the extra mile to meet each other's needs.
- We competently use our authority.

Innovative

- We encourage the expression of new ideas.
- We willingly try new ideas.
- We practice the philosophy, "Mistakes are learning opportunities for competence building."

Teamwork

- We understand what we need from each other.
- We proactively meet the needs of others to help each other to be successful.
- We recognize each other for jobs well done.
- We use consensus when making team decisions.

Open Communication

- We present the facts of the situation.
- We feel free to express our ideas.
- We objectively accept diverse ideas.
- We openly discuss the behaviors to be implemented to improve teamwork.

Trust

- We are dependable and do what we agree to do.
- We keep confidential information confidential.
- We keep each other informed with the necessary information.
- We are consistent so team members know what to expect from each other.

Respect

- We recognize and accept our individual differences.

- We listen to and understand input.
- We use input whenever possible.
- We tell each other how their input was used.

Accountability

- We competently complete our job responsibilities.
- We competently complete our responsibilities in support of the team's decisions.
- We provide each other feedback regarding the progress of meeting each other's needs.
- We accept the feedback offered to improve performance.
- We do what needs to be done to implement the Team-Work Values Statement.

People Operating System: Among Members of the Work Unit

Putting this statement to work means meeting the challenge to institutionalize these behaviors within the people operating system. The basic process begins with senior-level work units as a demonstration that top-down change produces bottom-up commitment.

The president of The Cole Company, Kevin, began implementing the systematic process to improve the efficiency of working relationships within their people operating system. He and the vice presidents collected baseline measurements based on their TeamWork Values Statement to quantify the efficiency of their working relationships. The data showed that members of his work unit were not proactively meeting each other's needs for the success of the plant. While discussing the data, several managers expressed frustration about the apparent apathy about doing what needs to be done to help each other to be more successful. These managers noted that peers are great at making commitments to assist each other, but these quickly become a memory upon leaving their staff meeting. These managers identified the following six potential behavioral solutions that would be apparent if they were more efficiently cooperating with each other:

1. Demonstrate a willingness to learn when a colleague needs our assistance.
2. Negotiate a time frame as to when the assistance could be made available.
3. Schedule a Tuesday and Thursday team coordination meeting to identify what each manager needs from each other.
4. Proactively assist each other whenever possible.
5. Provide each other immediate feedback when needs are not being met.
6. Involve affected colleagues in the decision-making process.

The managers decided to implement numbers 1, 2, 4, and 5. These behavioral strategies were loaded into the software, and Kevin and his team focused on implementing and measuring the success of each strategy.

Paul is a manager within The Cole Company, and his work unit consists of several very energetic, assertive, verbal, and strongly opinionated individuals. A scheduled one-hour meeting would often continue for several hours. The baseline data showed they did a lackluster job of listening to each other without interrupting. These turf warriors were too busy preparing a response to defend their position rather than trying to understand their colleagues.

This work unit elected to implement the following five behavioral strategies with a great deal of measured success:

*   Schedule more one-on-one time with each other to discuss specific issues.
*   Remain quiet to listen to the team member speaking.
*   Remind each other to let other members finish their thoughts.

- Keep focused on the subject being discussed.
- Provide immediate feedback on the success of using these strategies.

The measurement process simply provided the tool for the work unit to address the issue that historically had been quietly eroding its efficiency.

Cole Company's TeamWork Values Statement states that the team's decisions are based on a consensus of its members. Shelvie's work unit found that putting these words into practice was more of a challenge than writing them into a statement. The data from the work unit indicated that her work unit leaders frequently did not have input into decisions that affected them or their respective departments. Either Shelvie would make the decision in isolation, or two or more work unit leaders would make decisions independently while knowing that the decision would have an impact on other departments. These decisions were not made to be malicious. Rather they simply reflected the business culture that was allowed to flourish.

Needless to say, the work environment was a frustrating one for the affected managers left out of the communication loop. Moreover, valuable time was wasted as a result of the fragmented working relationships and ineffective coordination that stymied efficient completion of job responsibilities. In short, too much time was spent discussing the frustrations about being left out of the communication loop. These frustrations were clearly costing the company money, as is always the case. This group of leaders implemented the following strategies to ensure that decisions benefited from the affected manager's input.

- Staff meetings are to be used as the conduit to discuss issues that impact multiple leaders.
- If a leader initiates an activity involving two or more departments, their peers are to ensure that affected people are represented in the process.
- Each leader identifies instances in which they did not have input.

- Each leader is responsible to present these instances at the next weekly staff meeting.
- If a decision must be made without an affected leader's input, then that individual is so notified as quickly as possible, with an explanation for making the decision without that input.

Measuring the use of these strategies enables these leaders to integrate them into their day-to-day operations. As is often the case, these leaders were aware of this pattern of dysfunctional teamwork behavior, but the issue was not addressed until a system to improve the working relationships was put in place. In effect, the system to measure behavior was the communication tool that opened the door to discuss their dysfunctional behaviors and successfully apply solutions. If The Cole Company had not initiated the effort to improve teamwork, the negative team behaviors adversely impacting working relationships would likely have been left unattended, acting as a thief to steal valuable resources.

People Operating System: Interdepartmental or Between Work Units

Working relationships with internal customers is another major category included within the people operating system. In theory, each department exists to help other departments be successful, or, put it another way: "Your priorities are our priorities when you need our assistance." In practice, the proverbial silo structure frequently emerges and walls are constructed preventing departments from helping each other to maximize each other's performance. The operational rule becomes, "I'm too busy fighting my alligators to even think about helping you fight yours."

Accepting the responsibility that each department exists to help its internal customers to be successful requires reliance on the same systematic team building process.

- Measure the extent to which the behaviors contained in the TeamWork Values Statement are being used between departments to quantify the baseline strengths, and identifying opportunities to improve the respective working relationships.
- Define and implement strategies to improve those behaviors that need strengthening.
- Measure the impact of these strategies.

In this instance, the respective department manager rates the degree they think their department works with their internal customers who, in turn, measure the degree the department implements the TeamWork Values Statement while working with them.

Keith has been the human resources leader at Cole Company for over ten years. Other managers complained to the president about the lack of support from human resources for several years, so it was no surprise when the data showed a need for the human resources area to better understand the needs of departments. Based on these data, this peer group defined the following five behaviors needed from the human resources department to help them be more successful:

1. Immediately initiate recruiting for open positions.
2. Keep other work unit leaders informed as to the status of the recruiting effort.
3. Provide a more direct answer to peer group questions.
4. Discuss proposed procedural changes with other management staff before implementing.
5. Document the final changes to ensure understanding.

Measuring behavior addressed a longstanding problem and provided the tool for human resources to become a more effective member of the management team instead of an irritating source of frustration.

In another instance, the measured perception was that the quality department was not proactively meeting the needs of other departments to help them be more successful. Working with this data, the other work unit leaders asked Dave, the quality work unit leader, to:

- Be more available to his staff in the production areas to review his staff's efforts to complete their job responsibilities.
- Do what needs to be done *now,* to demonstrate a sense of urgency.
- Work with other managers to identify improvement projects that would have a positive impact upon the quality of the finished product.
- Keep managers informed as to the status of working quality improvement initiatives.

In this instance, these managers elected to rate the quality department on a weekly basis since these behaviors were so crucial to the plant's operations. Measured feedback showed a marked improvement and helped the quality department to become a more integral and respected component of Cole Company's operations.

In Closing

As the examples in this chapter illustrate, using data is a powerful communication tool to address people issues that have historically eroded the working relationships. Data allowed the individuals involved in the preceding examples to convert frustration into energy to improve working relationships. These examples provide testimony to the facts that *frustration is your best friend*® and that what gets measured improves. Let's now turn our attention to the third element of the people operating system: the working relationship between employees and their supervisor.

7 | The Teacher Becomes the Student

In the preceding chapter we discussed two of the three basic components of the people operating system: the working relationship among members of the work unit and between work units. This chapter introduces the third basic component: the working relationship between employees and their work unit leader. Work unit leaders have more of an impact upon their employees' loyalty to the company, morale, and productivity than they may readily recognize.

Buckingham and Coffman reported in their book *First, Break All the Rules* that "the team leader, not the pay, benefits, perks or a charismatic corporate leader, was the critical player in building a strong workplace." These authors have documented the fact that it is better to work for a great leader in an old-fashioned work environment than for a bad leader in a work environment that supports employee participation. Our work supports the position that the work unit leader is responsible for creating a psychological environment that encourages people to be creative and productive, and to enjoy their work environment.

There is considerable pressure on the work unit leader to perform. Traditionally that pressure has been to be highly productive and profitable. The people track that we're discussing represents another pressure point. Today's leader is expected to demonstrate both technical and people competencies.

People Operating System: Between Work Unit Leader and Their Employees

The high-performing leader understands the operating principle that *the perception held by others can be more important than their self-perception.* For that reason such leaders strive to maximize their effectiveness by wanting to know how members of their work unit perceive them walking the talk of the TeamWork Values Statement. For example, suppose your perception is that you work to meet the needs of others, but those working with you think you don't. Who is correct? Everything you do is seen through their eyes of your not being cooperative, so you're not. To maximize human potential you must know the relationship between self-perception and the perception of others. Knowing that allows you to capitalize upon your strengths and improve those behaviors that can be adding frustration to the working relationships.

The systematic process to improve the leader's performance is identical to the one we used to improve the working relationships within and between work units.

- Measure the degree the work unit leader is walking the talk of the TeamWork Values Statement to identify behavioral strengths and those that need to be strengthened. For the work unit leader to see himself or herself through the eyes of the employees requires obtaining that information from employees. In this instance the leader rates herself or himself and employees rate the leader.
- The raters then define behavioral solutions designed to improve the work unit leader's performance.
- The raters measure the work unit leader's success to implement the solutions.

- Continuously monitor the work unit leader's performance and work with additional behavioral solutions as needed.

Collecting data to determine the degree of alignment between the leader's behaviors and the TeamWork Values Statement can be more sensitive than rating a work unit's use of these behaviors. The individual is put under the spotlight, so to speak. Work unit leaders want to be perceived as doing a good job, and measuring their performance can threaten their ego. Consequently, you may become a little uptight when your behaviors are discussed within this context. Feeling uncomfortable is part of your natural defense mechanism to protect you from being hurt. The challenge for you is to override the protection provided by this psychological immunity system and be willing to see the as-is situation. The antidote to override your natural defenses is an open mind. The willingness to accept the pain of the truth allows you to see the truth. Seeing the truth is the only way for you to improve your performance. We return to this subject in chapter 13.

Let's return to The Cole Company. Tricia, an engineering supervisor, was surprised when the data showed that her employees thought she lacked consistency when establishing priorities. She initially thought that her employees were not interpreting the question set correctly. Through discussing the data she learned that her employees did not know from one day to the next what specific tasks they would be assigned to complete. These employees silently evoked a twenty-four-hour rule upon receiving instructions, because these instructions would probably change tomorrow. Fortunately, she was ultimately willing to accept the data and agreed to implement strategies to bring order to the chaos she was creating. Tricia and her staff decided to implement the following three corrective action steps:

1. Establish the priorities for the engineering projects and the associated timelines at the weekly staff meeting.

2. Any adjustments to these priorities are made at the regularly scheduled staff meeting, if it all possible.
3. Emergency adjustments to the priority schedule are made after obtaining input from the staff who would be responsible for completing to task.

Individuals must fix themselves, and the subsequent measurements showed that Tricia reduced the frustrations in the working relationships by successfully implementing the defined strategies.

Another one of The Cole Company's leaders, Larry, was overusing his authority to go the extra mile to meet other work unit's needs. Larry, in the spirit of cooperation, frequently committed the work unit to assist other work units without taking into consideration the existing workload. The members of his work unit wanted to be cooperative with other departments, but often felt overwhelmed with the responsibilities to complete their job requirements while at the same time taking on the extra load. The members simply wanted to have the opportunity to provide input into the commitment.

The defined solutions that were used to improve Larry's performance were simply to

• Discuss potential commitments with the work unit whenever possible.
• Use his employees' feedback regarding the magnitude of their workload.
• Adjust existing priorities to incorporate the new commitments.

Our final example is Debbie, a well-liked, long-term employee who was promoted to customer service supervisor. Shortly after her promotion, her staff learned about a different Debbie. She did not trust her staff to work independently of her supervision. She told them what to do, how to do it, and when to do it. Plus, she towered over her employees to watch them complete their responsibilities whenever possible. As expected, the data confirmed her reputation. She and the staff generated the following four behavioral solutions:

1. Define the results to be achieved.
2. Give her staff members the authority to achieve the defined results.
3. Allow the staff the freedom to complete their responsibilities.
4. Remove herself from watching her employees complete their responsibilities.

Subsequent measurements showed marked improvement in Debbie's behavior, and her staff began to enjoy their work again.

A Communication Tool

Work unit leaders obviously have a tremendous impact upon the quality of life of their employees. High-performing leaders understand the consequences associated with their behaviors and are committed to create a workplace environment that fosters loyalty, creativity, and high performance. The bottom line is that high-performing leaders want to do what is necessary so their employees enjoy working with them as an individual and the organization as a whole.

Data opens the door for employees to discuss behaviors with their supervisor. In the preceding instances, the behaviors that were identified as needing improvement existed before data were collected. But nothing was done, because in the absence of a system to improve working relationships, the employees felt as though they did not have permission to discuss the behaviors openly. Instead, they complained to each other. Data makes behaviors more empirical, and implementing a system to improve working relationships can be the key to discuss needed improvements.

Putting the data to work is the most effective tool for the work unit leader to demonstrate commitment for personal improvement. The magic of the work unit leader's touch through their behaviors can work wonders to have a positive impact upon morale, production, and profits. Everything the work unit leader does, does not do, says, or does not say sends a message, and all eyes and ears are listening.

360° Performance Evaluation

We would be amiss to not discuss the popular 360° multi-rater process, because it certainly can be an effective developmental tool to improve individual interpersonal performance, which serves as the common denominator for the working relationships contained within the people operating system.

For those readers not familiar with this process, an individual rates himself/herself on a set of characteristics, and the supervisor rates the individual, as do some peers and other employees (in some instances, other stakeholders are also included). The data are presented so the individual can compare one's own self-rating versus that of the 360° team members.

The 360° multi-rater assessment can be easily included in the organization's arsenal to help individuals implement their TeamWork Values Statement. Unfortunately, this powerful tool is acquiring a negative reputation because it is not being used effectively—another example of a good system getting a bad rap when the people misusing the tool deserve the rap on the knuckles. The root cause for this misuse is the lack of a systematic process to improve performance.

For example, we're aware of instances in which a given employee was on more than thirty 360° teams and given a time frame of two weeks to complete a forty-five-minute questionnaire per individual. The 360° team members were simply overworked for a short period of time. The validity of the data had to be suspect when using such a procedure.

The most frequent complaint is how the data are used, or should we say not used. The participant receives a report that is reviewed and promptly placed on the shelf. Sometimes this report is made available weeks and even months after the data were collected. Both instances represent a waste of data, not to mention the waste of time to collect the data and money paid to the vendor. The psychological message communicated in this environment is not one conducive to personal improvement. The problem is magnified when the individual is given the data in the personal report and told s/he is expected to improve the numbers by next year without any support on how to convert the data into action plans.

We're obviously not the only ones being confronted with such tragedies. David Antonioni reported in his article "Designing an Effective 360-Degree Appraisal Feedback Process" that

- Specific goals or action plans are not being developed based on the feedback.
- Individuals were left on their own to figure out how to improve their low scores.
- Most of the immediate team leaders failed to follow up on action plans that were defined.
- Most of those rated felt their team leader did not recognize their efforts to improve their work behaviors.

There is a better way.

To maximize the benefits associated with the 360° multi-rater process, the data must be converted into a behavior change and must provide immediate feedback to effectively reinforce the behavior change. Once the 360° team members are identified, the systematic process to put the data to work is identical to that already discussed:

- The question set associated with the TeamWork Values Statement is used to obtain the baseline measurements to identify strengths and opportunities to improve the individual's performance.
- Once the baseline is established, the raters define solutions to improve personal performance.

- The team members then rate the degree to which the individual uses these solutions.

To maximize the return on your financial and psychological investment to use the 360° improvement process, the data need to be available in real time, as provided by the use of the MBC Software® methodologies. Not only does that availability provide more valid information, but it provides the necessary immediate feedback to reinforce behavior change.

By this time you know that we are proponents of an open learning environment. The 360° process is no exception. The data are available to be reviewed by the individual's immediate up-line team leader, because the up-line team leader is part of the faculty to help improve the individual's behavior. To be an effective teacher, this individual needs to see the data, help formulate solutions, monitor progress, and hold the process accountable. After all up-line supervisors have access to all the down-line technical data, the same open environment can be implemented with the people operating system as well. Data not being made available to the up-line team leader would be analogous to asking a sightless person to drive a car.

In support of the open learning environment, we encourage those who participated in the rating to also assist in developing improvement strategies. These individuals can be very effective teachers in providing valuable suggestions for improvement. Psychologically the 360° team members need to see that their input was used to reinforce the organizational perception that the 360° process is an important developmental tool.

Here's a case in point. Cheryl is a talented work unit employee at The Cole Company, but she was on a path of self-destruction and was quickly acquiring the reputation of

- Not listening to other employees.
- Demonstrating outbursts of anger.
- Overusing the proverbial "I" or "My team" statements that were seemingly sending the message that

other teams were not contributing as much to the organization's success as she or her department were contributing.

Her supervisor wanted to salvage this talented individual because she contributed to turning around a rather poorly performing department. A 360° team was created to assist her. As expected the baseline TeamWork Values Statement data showed opportunities to improve in remaining emotionally calm and listening for understanding. The 360° team defined the following six strategies for her to improve performance:

1. Hold one conversation at a time.
2. Listen without interrupting.
3. Maintain eye contact while listening.
4. Listen to understand the other person's point of view.
5. Accept the other person's point of view.
6. Remain in emotional control by refraining from outbursts of anger.

Both the quantitative data (team ratings) and qualitative data (verbal reports) showed that this employee made considerable progress. At the time of this writing, the 360° team is scheduled to rate her performance for the next two quarters and then terminate the process if her behavior stabilizes.

In Closing

We've completed our discussion on the basic components of the people operating system to measure and monitor the working relationships among members of the work unit, between work units, and between the work unit leader and employees. These systems allow you to review data on a regularly scheduled basis to develop your people assets that are analogous to the systems used to develop your technical assets.

The remainder of the book is designed to show you how to integrate these people systems into your management systems, the personal skills required to take advantage of these systems, and what these systems can do for your organization into the future.

8 | Meeting the Challenges of Using a Data-Based People Operating System

In spite of the tremendous potential to use real-time data for the people operating systems and organizational development, eight specific issues need to be addressed:

1. The use of ordinal data versus interval data.
2. The problem of rating the work unit as a unit.
3. Ease of collecting data.
4. Confidentiality and honesty of the data.
5. The process of putting the data to work.
6. Having an open system so the up-line supervisor can see data.
7. The willing participation of a team leader.
8. Accountability as a key to improving working relationships.

Ordinal Versus Interval Data

Data associated with the technical characteristics of the organization's performance has a decided advantage over the data associated with people operating systems. Technical measurements are based on interval data—that is, a physical measurement system. Interval data has a true zero, so the measurements are precise. For example, a profit margin of fifty cents is twice the margin of twenty-five cents. An error rate of 10 percent is twice that of 5 percent. When a machine is operating at 70 percent capacity, you know the precise dollars being lost because of poor performance.

In contrast, an ordinal scale of measurement is subjective because the number generator is a person, and we don't really know what the numbers mean. For example, suppose two people rated a team's performance a "3" on a six-point Likert Scale. There is no way of knowing if the same rating means the same performance level. In reality, one person may actually have perceived the rating as a "1" and inflated their rating. There is simply no way to get inside of people's heads to obtain the exact criterion used to rate performance.

Admittedly, ordinal data presents some disadvantages, but we just have to understand and accept the limitations. The lack of preciseness prevents comparing numbers. Suppose Work Unit A had a mean rating of "4" compared to Work Unit B with a rating of "2". The temptation is to say Work Unit A is performing twice as well as B. But that comparison violates the statistical assumptions for ordinal data. In reality, there are numerous reasons that a difference could exist between the ratings, and these reasons may not relate to level of performance. Suppose the raters in Work Unit A were afraid to rate honestly or had just celebrated a success and were in an extremely good mood when measuring their performance. These opposite energy forces yield the same result: inflated scores. The net result is that different individuals in the two work units used completely different criteria when entering their data. The temptation to compare ordinal data must be resisted, because any conclusions based on this comparison can be erroneous. The most important comparison is within the work unit from one measurement to another to know if the perceived performance is improving or not.

A common corporate practice is to compare the ordinal data of one work unit against a corporate profile. Such a comparison is interesting, but statistically meaningless. Suppose the work unit has an overall mean less than the corporate mean. The conclusion may be made that its performance is below the average corporate profile when in reality the exact opposite may be the as-is situation. The temptation to make such comparisons using ordinal data is created by the relative ease of being able to do so with interval data. For example, if your work unit had a profit that is more than the corporate average, then you can conclude that your financial performance is higher by some percent than the corporate profile. Making conclusions that a location or department is better or worse than a corporate average cannot be made with ordinal data. We can never know the extent of erroneous conclusions or the damage done by the inappropriate use of ordinal data.

Rating the Work Unit As a Whole

Rating the work unit as a whole is admittedly more challenging than measuring an individual. The difficulty emerges when some members of the work unit are using the behavior, *"We exhibit dependability by doing what we agree to do,"* quite well while others are struggling. The challenge is to decide upon a rating that represents the range of variability in the work unit. Although these measurements represent a psychological challenge, that data is easier to work with because it does not highlight a given individual. For that reason, we use this as the starting point to help the employees learn how to use data and to demonstrate that data can be used in a constructive manner to promote honesty when rating behaviors before rating individuals.

Ease of Collecting Data

Ease of collecting data represents another advantage of technical measurements; they are relatively easy to collect, and data are usually available on a regular schedule. The data for the people operating systems must likewise be easily collected. The fact that data are entered from the privacy of a computer when using an electronic performance support system facilitates the ease of data collection, but the amount of time to enter the data is another issue. Once users are familiar with operating the software, it takes approximately five minutes to enter data associated with a twenty- to twenty-five-item questionnaire. Less time is required to quantify solutions, which usually reduces the question set to three to seven behaviors. The concern about time is usually not a major issue, but the data entry must be easy.

The frequency of data collection also needs to be considered. The frequency of entering data is dependent upon a number of factors. When collecting baseline data, it needs to be collected as quickly as possible to measure the as-is situation. We often collect data once or twice weekly in an effort to prevent the baseline data from being confounded by other issues that tend to occur as these measurements are spread over time.

We're not working with a perfect science on the plant floor, so we work within the confines of the existing environment. Although we prefer the consistency of regularly scheduled data entry, that goal is not always possible. The real world dictates operating in a less than perfect environment, and some data are better than no data at all.

Other issues that impact the frequency of data collection are the set of strategies being implemented and the maturity of the work unit. Some work units opt to enter data weekly as the data entry serves as a reminder for them to implement their TeamWork Values Statement. Once the strategies have been stabilized, the data entry can be scheduled less frequently to ensure that the strategies have been institutionalized within the work group.

The important issue is consistency in using the data. You have a consistent schedule to use technical measurements—numbers associated with production, budget, inventory, and safety—and that schedule is determined by the need to put the data to work and to make the necessary changes to ensure high performance. The data associated with the people operating system should be reviewed with the same requirements: consistency in accordance with a schedule to ensure high performance.

Honest Data

Honesty is always the best policy. Can you imagine anyone purposely telling a physician the wrong symptoms or providing only a partial list of symptoms? We've discussed the chaos that would exist if numbers describing the as-is technical characteristics were nonexistent, and that same chaos would exist if you could not trust the honesty of the numbers. Without honest numbers, managing the processes would not be possible. As a matter of fact, large sums of money are spent obtaining sophisticated tracking systems to ensure having the necessary data to manage the technical characteristics profitably.

Honesty also applies to the people operating system. Accurate numbers offer the only way to identify the as-is strengths and opportunities of the working relationships composing the people operating system.

The issue of confidentiality is at the heart of honest data. The users must feel that a security net protects them from allowing anyone to learn of their individual ratings. That is the obvious advantage of completing a paper-and-pencil assessment, which is then sent to a third party to score and prepare the results. The obvious disadvantage with that approach is the time delay between collecting the data and the opportunity to review it. The MBC Software® methodology eliminates that disadvantage, but introduces the suspicion that "someone may find out an individual's rating." Working with an electronic behavioral support system has shown this suspicion can be minimized once the employees understand the mechanics of the software.

Unfortunately employees are driven by fear to not be honest. Just consider the irony of this fact. We encourage our employees to be dishonest because of the way we work with each other. We can't count the number of times we've heard employees admit to withholding negative information, because "the messenger gets killed in this organization." Kathleen Ryan and Daniel Oestreich, in their book *Driving Fear Out of the Workplace,* reported that 70 percent of employees are afraid to be honest in the workplace, and the fear of reprisal is the primary factor driving that fear. Even when the fear subsides of finding out how individuals rated, the fear remains that low ratings will not be received favorably. Frankly, sometimes that is the case. For example, we had a plant manager who mentioned to his team, upon observing a series of low ratings, that evidently someone is not happy with the working relationships and they need to either speak up or to see him in private. Needless to say, the low rating went away, driven away by the plant manager's reaction. To his credit, the manager realized he had erred. In this particular case, we were able to use this as a learning opportunity. First, the plant manager admitted to the error. Second was the opportunity to show the members of the team how their behaviors impacted others and the importance of accepting the data at face value.

The human tendency to rate performance a little higher than what you really think it ought to be is another characteristic that needs to be addressed. Obviously, this tendency is exacerbated when fear is present or the rater suspects the data will not remain confidential or be used properly. You cannot control the degree of fear any given individual may happen to harbor. You can certainly use behaviors that encourage honesty. First is the sincere appreciation for honest data. Second is to put the data to work to improve the people operating systems, as discussed in the next section.

Put the Data to Work

Employees are so accustomed to good ideas being put to rest in the idea-of-the-month cemetery that many are very doubtful about the lasting effort to improve working relationships. This fact speaks to the issue of top-down change producing bottom-up commitment and institutionalizing a systems approach to encouraging a behavior change. A common neck ailment exists in every organization, caused by employees at every organizational level looking up to see what the senior leaders are doing. Seeing is believing, which creates the opportunity to cascade the improvement process throughout the organization.

Employees need to see that up-line employees are in fact implementing the measurement system to improve the efficiency of the people operating systems as well as the improvements in interpersonal behaviors as a consequence of putting the data to work.

An Open Data System

The intent is to implement an electronic performance support system for the people operating systems that parallels that used for the technical operating systems. In the typical organizational alignment, the top-level manager has access to all the data associated with the technical characteristics throughout the organization. A given work unit has access to the necessary data to manage its own performance, and these data are also available to up-line supervisors. We are likewise proponents of an open data system with the people operating systems. Obviously the work unit or individual must have the necessary data to manage one's own performance. By now, you know we're advocates for the up-line supervisors having access to their respective down-line data. The CEO has access to data throughout the user network.

Some readers may likely cringe or at least take exception to this approach, as traditional multi-rater procedures only allow up-line managers access to the data upon the discretion of the person being rated. We consider the up-line supervisor as part of the faculty to teach and monitor the use of the TeamWork Values Statement, which requires full access to the data. We address the requirements to be an effective teacher in a later chapter, but for now let's accept the fact that the teacher needs access to the appropriate data to hold students accountable, who in this case are their down-line supervisors and work units.

Willing Participation of the Work Unit Leader

When the top management position—for example, CEO, president, or plant manager—is an unwilling participant, implementing the people operating systems in the organization is more of a challenge. Under these circumstances, those staff reporting to the top manager must really be committed. A typical scenario is a mid-level work unit manager who is reluctant to participate in the process to improve working relationships, as illustrated in the following examples.

In one situation, an individual verbalized a willingness to participate in the organizational effort to institutionalize their TeamWork Values Statement. The willingness was not converted into a behavior change. This work unit leader was perceived to be intimidating and did not appreciate input from staff, considering a staff meeting as a waste of time. His stated philosophy was to tell team members only what they needed to know to do their job. The work unit leader quickly surmised that the low ratings provided by employees were wrong.

The most effective procedure to work with this reluctance is to engage the participation of their immediate supervisor, but that meeting was a dismal failure. The president agreed the work unit leader needed to change, but promptly announced, "That individual reports to the corporate staff with a dotted line to me, so the teamwork issue is their problem." The bottom line was that we could not help this work unit, and the members continued to suffer the wrath of their ineffective leader.

Now, a success story with almost the same scenario as we've been discussing: a very intimidating team leader who expressed the perception of promoting very efficient teamwork. The data showed that not to be the case, to the point that several team members expressed an unwillingness to participate in the improvement process.

This situation was brought to the attention of the plant manager, who agreed to work with the team leader in question. The data showed the pattern of a micromanaging manager. The raters defined the following strategies, which were ultimately used successfully by the manager:

- The staff had input into decisions that affected them.
- The staff were given the authority to make independent decisions.
- The staff made recommendations whenever a problem was presented to the manager.

Three choices are available when working with a reluctant team leader. The first one focuses on change by incorporating the up-line supervisor as the teacher to hold the person accountable for change. This level of cooperation is crucial to successfully change behavior. The second is to accept the fact nothing is going to be done. Obviously, the higher in the organizational chart this option has to be used, the more damage that can be done by the individual's interpersonal incompetence. Third, the reluctant work unit manager who sends the message that he or she does not want to be a participant in the new culture should be given the opportunity to be recycled, to go elsewhere and find the organization where he or she might be a better fit.

Accountability Is a Key

Accountability is simply doing what is expected. That requires everyone to understand the behaviors to be implemented within your company. In this instance, these behaviors are not only contained in your value statement, but the performance management system that is used to create the culture described in the TeamWork Values Statement. The importance of accountability cannot be overemphasized, and for that reason we discuss accountability in detail in chapter 11.

In Closing

At this point we've discussed the following four components of a performance operating system:

- Defined a TeamWork Values Statement to guide the development of working relationships.
- Implemented an ongoing measurement system to manage the three basic working relationships within the people operating system.
- Defined, implemented, and measured strategic behavioral solutions/strategies to drive the improvement in working relationships.
- Ongoing monitoring and improvement of the working relationships.

The basic components of the people systems are in place, but the major challenges are yet to come, through the process of integrating the people operating system into your organizational culture. We begin the change process in the next chapter.

Part Three
CHANGE

9 | You Decide If Resistance Will Be Your Friend or Your Enemy

Organizations change when people change. Improving the efficiency of the people operating systems requires two sets of changes. First is the performance system underwriting the change effort, and second is the change in attitudes and behavior. You already know that you have more control over changing the performance system components than you do changing an individual's behavior. Not having direct control of a person's behavior creates a tremendous challenge while working to implement your TeamWork Values Statement within the people operating systems.

Research shows that 70 percent of corporate change efforts fail within the first eighteen months. The main reason for these failures is people not changing. That's the bad news. The good news is that your organization can be one of those that succeed—if you understand the change process and manage it effectively.

People Are the Gatekeepers for Change

The one bit of information that everyone seems to understand about change is that it is resisted. Common sense tells us that everyone should welcome with open arms the forthcoming improvements in working relationships. Logic also tells us that is not the case.

Think of resistance as the organizational immunity system. Change represents a strange virus that the organization works to rid itself of, in a manner similar to when our body works to remove foreign germs and viruses. Our bodies send antibodies to the rescue while organizations send people. Organizations don't resist change, people do that. Actually, it's not the change per se that is resisted, but the consequences of the change that are the focus of the resistance. Remembering this dynamic is very important. Change is perceived as good when the consequences are perceived to be good. The challenge is to help individuals understand the positive consequences associated with the change effort. Our intention is to capitalize on this resistance and use its energy to keep the change effort on the right track. When you understand that these individuals offering resistance are telling you that they are both interested in and experiencing the change process, then their resistance can become a positive event.

The Elements of Resistance

In the case of any given individual, the motivation for his or her resistance emerges from one or more of the following five elements.

1. *Inertia—"staying in the comfort zone" or "taking the path of least resistance" (some call it "the path of least persistence").*

Our bodies prefer to remain in a state of homeostasis—the status quo or the comfort zone—free of any tension. Natural human inclination is to prefer what is easy, and change usually requires some degree of extra effort. You can easily demonstrate that by folding your arms. Does your left or right arm go over the top? Now fold your arm with the other one on top. Feel uncomfortable? It's not natural. So you continue to do that which is comfortable.

Despite some degree of frustration inherent in the status quo, its predictability provides a certain security that can serve as a powerful damper on any impulse or energy to try something new. How many times have you heard that a given work unit or individual is known for not cooperating, and the words of the day are, "It's just easier to leave them alone than to try to encourage them to cooperate with us"? The frequently cited root cause for the existence of this mentality is that "at least we know what to expect."

An often-cited reason for not engaging in a systematic process to improve working relationships is the time and effort involved in the process. Would you agree that the time or work required to improve working relationships is a logical reason for *not* improving teamwork? Again, the lazy way out is to put up with the status quo.

2. *Fear of the Future.*

What's really going to happen? The truth of the matter is that many unknowns are present when implementing the TeamWork Values Statement. Some of these unknowns are:

- What happens if we're not successful?
- Will this effort be another entrant into the organizational cemetery?
- Will leaders walk the talk of the statement?
- What do we do if a leader does not cooperate with the effort?
- Are we capable of teaching the TeamWork Values Statement?
- Can we hold people accountable for implementing the change process?
- Our organization has a history of not doing a good job of working with people. Can we institutionalize the

practice of helping each other to be more successful?

- What happens if we create expectations that working relationships will be improved and then this balloon of excitement is burst, followed by yet another disappointment?

All these potential realities of the change process must be recognized, but they do not have to derail the improvement process.

3. Personal Consequences.

What's in it for me? What do I stand to gain or lose? It's only natural for people to think first of the personal consequences associated with the efforts to improve working relationships. The survival instinct continues to live.

In particular, any hint of a threat to one's financial security, a change in job title, or a lessening of one's power makes most people extremely uncomfortable. We're reminded of a team leader who may very well have been off the charts for using autocratic and dictatorial behaviors. He perceived the team-building effort to threaten his power base. He demonstrated this resistance by either being late or failing to attend meetings with his work unit to work on behavioral strategies for improvement. Numerous coaching sessions with him failed to produce any significant changes in his attitudes and behaviors. The old-fashioned process of delegating authority to his supervisors was simply not going to happen. He loved his power and flaunted it with every opportunity.

An integral component of personal consequences is the fear of losing control. We have a need to be in control of our destiny. The process of implementing the TeamWork Values Statement can be viewed by some as losing their personal identity instead of the proactive effort of creating a teamwork culture. Questions have been raised about "robotizing" and robbing employees of their individual identities. Obviously, that's not the case. The intent is to implement standard operating procedures for the people track, as they exist for the technical track.

4. *Change Produces Considerable Confusion.*

Because conflicting forces are operating, change is a dynamic energy system. The interaction of its opposing energy sources and the resulting confusion can be summarized in one question: "Do we continue the organizational change effort or terminate the process?" Confusion is another source of discomfort that can hack away at the energy sources driving change.

5. *Change Is Legitimately Not Needed*

Some people honestly believe that the organization would be best left as is. The company is profitable and people seem to get along reasonably well, so why introduce yet another process to create some organizational stress? After all "if it ain't broke, don't fix it."

The Two Faces of Resistance

Before discussing the strategies for dealing with these issues, we need to point out that resistance appears in two forms, active and passive.

1. *Active Resistance.*

Active resistance often takes the form of griping, groaning, and predictions of doom and usually sounds something like this:

- "Oh no, here we go again."
- "We tried that before. If it didn't work then, it certainly won't work now."
- "If we just keep quiet, this too shall pass."
- "Since it's not going to work anyway, I'm certainly not going to participate."

Or it may take the form of a question:

- "What's the point of all this nonsense?"
- "Why are we changing something that's not broken?"
- "Why are we paying an expensive consultant when we can do this ourselves?"

The interesting fact about questions like these is that while on the one hand they may represent a polite form of signaling an individual's resistance, on the other hand they can be offered as legitimate questions by parties interested in facilitating the change process. We mention this in order to caution you not to interpret every skeptical comment or question raised about the change process as being a sign of resistance on the part of the questioner. These questions can be signaling the need for additional information.

Admittedly, active resistance can be uncomfortable. Work unit leaders may find it difficult to answer the questions and may even feel as though their personal integrity is being questioned. To complicate the matter, a work unit leader may likewise doubt the integrity of the change process and be seeking answers to the identical questions from one's leader. So a leader who is proactively supporting the change process to the employees may also be raising questions about its legitimacy, and that's not a comfortable position to be in.

2. *Passive Resistance.*

Passive resistance can be observed in performance slowdowns. Work unit members forget to enter data or stay away from meetings to review data and discuss how to improve working relationships, or if they are present, not participate in the discussions. In general, they are apathetic to the improvement process.

Ten Strategies for Using Resistance As a Positive Energy Source

1. Remaining As Is . . . Is No Option.

One of the major errors committed in the change process is not defining the compelling reasons that remaining in the comfort zone with the existing teamwork corporate culture is not an option. John Kotter—in his article, "Leading Change," in a *Harvard Business Review* issue about change—made the statement that "75 percent of the managers need to support the organizational change effort to be successful." The solidarity of agreement on the reasons that the status quo of the comfort zone is no longer an option garners the necessary energy to launch a successful change effort.

The lack of knowledge that we're addressing in this section becomes even more pronounced as you go down through the organizational hierarchy. This very important dynamic is often overlooked. Ample discussion may have occurred for the senior leaders to know what is going on, but those discussions have not taken place at other levels in the organization. Without having the benefit of this knowledge, many employees would quickly tell you that the money being paid to the high-priced consultants would be better spent on salaries, equipment, or additional employees. The lack of knowledge artificially creates resistance.

For these reasons, one of the first tasks is to identify the sources of frustrations in the working relationships and other reasons that drive the need for change. Obtain input from throughout the organization, and compile a common list of the brutal truths driving the need to improve working relationships. This list often includes such statements:

- Low morale—working here is not fun.
- We are beating each other up.
- Production levels are adversely affected by how we currently work together.

- Our jobs are more difficult to complete than they need to be.
- We're wasting a lot of money on people inefficiencies.
- Our existing practices waste a great deal of time.
- We must change to remain competitive and exist as a company.
- We have too much redundancy and continue to re-design the wheel.
- We lack cooperation and the synergy needed to reach our common goals.
- Employee turnover rate is out the ceiling.
- Crisis management is the rule rather than the exception.
- There is too much stress in our work, and we need to have more fun.
- Quality of product suffers because our working relationships are fragmented.
- Our team leaders are hammering on their people, trying to push them instead of leading them.
- There is too much fear operating in the system.
- We do not hold managers accountable for developing their people.
- We operate by the seat-of-our-pants principle when working with our people.
- The silo mentality is our way of doing business.

Also ask them to generate a list of the advantages of the as-is situation. Some management teams we've worked with didn't list any advantages. Those that did list advantages mentioned statements such as:

- We know what to expect.
- We are not required to do anything differently.
- We are comfortable with the present situation.
- The company is profitable.
- Staying the same is easier.

2. *Lock Onto the Vision.*

The next major event is to lock onto where you want your TeamWork Values Statement to take you. The second major error of omission in most major change efforts is not telling the masses where the change effort is leading. Everyone must see the value statement, because everyone is expected to live it.

Remember a time when you purchased an item that exceeded your budget? You made a decision that you must have that item. You could not live without it, and therefore you were willing to make the necessary financial sacrifices to make it a reality. The TeamWork Values Statement must play a similar role for your organization. It must be so good that the organization cannot live without it. As a magnet, it must create a very powerful positive energy force. Actually you want the magnetic pull to be so intense that the decision is made that it is absolutely imperative to create it.

You can increase the excitement and intensity of your statement to list the benefits associated with your values statement. Some of the benefits will undoubtedly be as follows:

- Improved teamwork increases productivity, which leads to increased profits.
- Increased cooperation and therefore teamwork synergy.
- People will be proud to work here, want to stay, and will brag to their friends about such a great workplace.
- Prospective employees will hear this bragging and ask to come to work here.
- Individuals will be respected for their knowledge and skill sets and given the authority to do their job.
- We'll have more fun at work.
- Our work will be so much easier.
- In the words of Dolly Parton, "When we enjoy our jobs, we don't have to come to work for the rest of our lives."

Again, compile a common list from throughout the organization. As you will see, this data can be very important to convert resistance to a positive energy source.

Also create a list of disadvantages associated with implementing your TeamWork Values Statement and the proposed management system. Disadvantages usually appear as follows:

- Employees have to learn and use another management system.
- Both extra time and work will be required.
- A significant financial commitment is required (consultants are expensive!).
- The effort to improve teamwork may become another idea-of-the-month.

3. *Expect Resistance.*

How could anyone in their right mind *not* want to improve teamwork and implement the company's TeamWork Values Statement?

You already know about five sources of resistance. Many of the behaviors you will see in your organization will look like the following:

Easier to remain as is. People will decide it is easier to remain as is than to take the time and work to define a Team-Work Values Statement, implement a measuring system, identify opportunities for improvement, define and implement teamwork strategies, and then quantify the progress made by these strategies. Paying lip service to improving teamwork is much easier than doing it.

The story of a vice president of a financial institution we were working with provides an excellent example of talking but not following through. The data showed that she needed to do a better job at holding members of her work accountable for completing their assignments in a timely fashion. Specific instances were identified in which the lack of accountability had allowed members of her staff to fall behind, resulting in major interruptions in the workflow. She agreed to hold everyone to established timelines, but her actions never followed the words. She became a victim of her own comfort zone. It was just easier not to exert the effort to hold people accountable.

Fear of the future. This source of resistance when implementing the TeamWork Values Statement often takes the form of not wanting to know the truth. Quite frankly, data associated with teamwork is more sensitive than the technical measurements. The teamwork data touches on issues of the ego, because everyone wants to think they are doing well regardless of their actual level of performance.

In one case, a production manager expressed a great deal of reluctance in beginning the process of measuring the extent to which members of his staff were implementing their TeamWork Values Statement. His reluctance was based on the concern that the data would confirm his suspicion that his work unit wasn't doing very well.

Concern over personal consequences. To begin with, some people perceive the effort to make improvements in the culture of the workplace as a personal affront, an implication that something is wrong with the way they are doing their jobs. We are reminded of a supervisor who upon learning about the organizational effort to improve teamwork immediately told everyone that he had been practicing teamwork for the past fifteen years and it was about time that the other supervisors caught up to him. He portrayed himself as an expert at teamwork and wondered aloud why others did not follow his practices. His bragging was the first clue that something was not quite right with his management style. In fact, he intimidated his team members to the point where they did not want to participate in defining teamwork strategies as a part of the team-building process. Job security can be a tremendous motivator, and he used it to his advantage.

The confusion of change. As you know, confusion can be frustrating. So the trick is to make confusion and frustration friends of the change process. When the data showed that members of the vice president's staff were not cooperating and several efforts to implement strategies to improve cooperation failed to produce measured success, the confusion about what to do became so intense that at one point someone suggested, "Let's just forget this teamwork stuff and continue beating up on each other."

Better for the organization not to change. "If it ain't broke, don't fix it." A very powerful source of resistance appears in such words as, "We're profitable, we get along with each other quite well, so let's leave well enough alone."

At the surface level, this approach appears to be a strong defense. The problem is that it is established on the old cliché: "If we continue to do that which we've always done, then we will always get what we've always gotten." That rule no longer applies in today's corporate communities. In today's world, if you're not sitting on the edge of your comfort zone, then you're taking up too much space.

4. The 20-60-20 rule.

As you listen to the resistance emerging from your organization you will find about 20 percent of a given team's members will immediately resist change, 20 percent will embrace it, and 60 percent will adopt a more cautious, wait-and-see attitude. These percentages may vary, of course, but these three distinct groups emerge.

An often-made mistake is to focus on the resisting force, in accordance with the "squeaky wheel" syndrome. You want to listen to it, work with it, and move on. All too often, vocal resisters receive too much attention. From their soapbox for attention, they receive a disproportionate amount of validity and legitimacy.

It's critical to discuss the fact that resistance is an integral component of the change process; even cite the 20-60-20 rule. Demonstrate that it's okay to be cautious about the process of change, to ask questions, and to voice skepticism. Use this educational forum to help everyone understand that resistance is a natural event and communicates the fact that the effort to improve teamwork is being felt. Remember that resistance is saying, "I'm not convinced yet," so ask what the person is objecting to, or doesn't understand, or what information is needed to convince him or her that the improved teamwork is needed. This dialogue is also a demonstration that people are indeed the organization's most important asset by empowering them to voice their input—which is an integral characteristic to improve communication within the organization. The important point is to structure the resisters' involvement and then move on.

The bulk of the attention needs to be addressed to the 20 percent who are eager to move the organization forward. Here are your informal leaders. Encourage their participation at every opportunity. Utilize them to help work with the resisters. Ensure they receive ample attention, for this group will be instrumental in encouraging the 60 percent group to enthusiastically participate in improving the teamwork culture. That 60 percent represents a critical mass to successfully improve the teamwork culture, so obviously you want the energy represented in this critical mass to support the change effort.

5. Design and implement change strategies.

Change can be talked to death. Ultimately, talk must be converted to action through defining and implementing teamwork strategies.

Management gurus offer differing opinions about how quickly change should be implemented. Advocates of continuous improvement support change in incremental steps. Reengineering proponents support a more massive change effort. The fact is that change can occur too slowly to demonstrate progress and momentum is lost, while at the same time change can occur so rapidly that it traumatizes. The key is to find the maximum speed for your organization.

6. The appearance of Murphy's Law.

So what else is new, right? Even when we've been fore-warned to expect them, difficulties and frustrations can be disappointing. For example, team members are not available to enter data or even forget to do so. The computer network fails when you want to enter data. The defined strategies either do not work or team members do not implement them. Finding time to review the data can be difficult in light of the technical challenges. The list goes on.

During such times, you may hear statements like, "See? I told you it wasn't going to work!" or, "This teamwork stuff is just too much hassle."

Here is a challenge for you. Instead of considering Murphy's Law the enemy, consider it as a teacher. Ask the question, "What is Murphy trying to teach us?"

- Discuss the sources of frustration, disappointment, and discouragement. They are okay. Such incidents occur every day in technical operations.
- Turn the incidents into positive events by identifying what was learned as the result of these experiences.

7. Lead by example.

Recently a CEO failed to rate himself for a period of several weeks. When asked why, he could only respond that he "got busy and forgot." His "absentmindedness" was extremely frustrating to members of his staff, more than one of whom asked, "Are we going to implement this teamwork stuff or not?"

Questioning what this glaring lack of commitment meant, the staff offered the following observations:

- They felt the CEO was shirking his responsibilities.
- It seemed clear that the CEO did not really care about improving working relationships within the organization.

- Perhaps the CEO did not want to face the issue that he had defined areas for improvement.
- People who had been excited about working on team-work issues were discouraged and disappointed by his behavior.

Whether work unit leaders like it or not, every word spoken or not spoken and action completed or not completed sends a very powerful message. Unfortunately, managers often overlook the awesome impact of their own reluctance to change. Not only do they become victims of their own habits, so do those they lead.

It takes guts to lead by example, because every action and word expressed represent leadership by example. Leadership by example to walk the talk of your TeamWork Values Statement and performance system can be one of your greatest challenges. It's always easier to voice the words of creating a desired working relationship than to convert these words to a behavior change.

8. Measure success.

Change must be measured to be seen. Nothing serves as a more effective antidote to resistance than measured success. Measured teamwork makes it tangible and more believable. Furthermore the measured success can be used to take advantage of the "looking up to see syndrome" operating within your organization. Down-line work units are more eager to participate after looking up and seeing the measured improvement of their senior work units.

9. Offer recognition for implementing change.

People need to be recognized for doing a job well. Provide psychological incentives for those under your direct control with the sincere expression of a few words—"Thank you" or "Great job!"

Ironically, such a powerful source as positive recognition is so easily overlooked when you consider the fact that you depend upon feedback throughout the course of the day with everything you do to measure the progress being achieved. Feedback is so crucial that you can't even dress for work or get to work without feedback showing the progress achieved.

Psychological feedback is especially important during times of change. The employees will be able to see the numbers and receive the feedback necessary to drive improvements in working relationships. But more than numbers are important. People want recognition for a job well done. They want to be winners, to be appreciated and applauded.

10. *Communicate, communicate, and communicate some more.*

Implementing a communication plan is a crucial element to successfully managing the change effort toward improving working relationships. Employees need to know:

- Why teamwork must be improved.
- The TeamWork Values Statement and the associated benefits.
- How each person will be affected.
- When success is achieved.
- The concerns, questions, and complaints about the process to improve the culture.
- What is being learned as the result of Murphy's Law walking around your corporate hallways.

Because top-down change produces bottom-up commitment, the CEO's leadership as the key spokesperson and model for change is important. Employees throughout the organization need to know the progress that senior work units are achieving, which can be achieved through publishing data and improvement strategies in a newsletter, on your intranet Web site, or at another conspicuous location.

Plus, the CEO and other senior managers need to fill the informal communication avenues with sounds of teamwork. That means talking about the implementation of the TeamWork Values Statement at the coffeepot, break rooms, cafeteria, and wherever they happen to be visiting with employees.

At the more formal level, the CEO needs to attend as many meetings as possible throughout the organization to send the message about the vision. For example, one of the CEOs with whom we worked conducted staff meetings at multiple locations at least once a year to discuss the TeamWork Values Statement. He made certain their value statement was an integral component of their leadership/management development courses. He wanted all employees to understand that people capital is a priority, and he consistently sent the message that creating and maintaining the culture described in their Team-Work Values Statement was an important priority.

The communication must start with the CEO, but it must not stop with the CEO. Other senior leaders need to carry this banner as well. These leaders need to meet with their downline work units to talk about their emerging culture and review the progress being made.

In Closing

Because resistance is an integral component of change, we want it to be a friend rather than its enemy. We've listed the major tools to be used to convert resistance into a positive energy source. Any tool is only successful when it is being used. We put these tools to work in the next chapter to improve your organizational IQ.

10 | Blueprints for Change

Change is a dynamic energy system containing opposing forces. The key to a successful change effort lies in understanding these forces and implementing systematic strategies to increase the energy encouraging change while minimizing the impact of the opposing energy.

In chapter 9 we discussed the five sources of resistance and the ten strategies for converting resistance into positive energy to support the change effort. This chapter presents the blueprints to use these ten strategies to successfully manage the energy forces interacting within each of the five stages of change.

Stage One: Identify Frustration

Frustration is your best friend® means that being dissatisfied with the status quo is the first prerequisite to improving working relationships. Dissatisfaction with the as-is situation provides the initial fuel for change. It pushes you to take action, as illustrated in Figure 1. Dissatisfaction is the energy source to push people out of complacency and their operational ruts created by how things were done yesterday.

Yesterday's ruts can become today's grave unless you become dissatisfied with how you worked together yesterday.

Figure 1

Identify Frustration

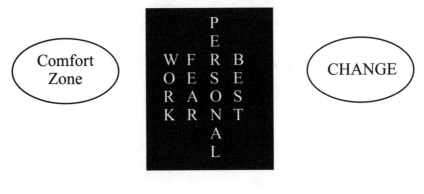

The Push of Frustration

Resistance

The decision to leave the old and create a new teamwork corporate culture has been made. You can rest assured that as soon as the word "change" is spoken, resistance will surface as demonstrated in Figure 2. Like a stone rolling down a hill, the resistance movement will gather momentum. You'll hear comments like:

- "If it's not broke, there is no need to fix it."
- "What will happen if we try it and it doesn't work?"
- "What do I have to do now?"
- "That consultant doesn't know what s/he's talking about."
- "Didn't we try something like that before?"
- "Nothing is going to change around here, because they

will keep the same old deadheads, and if you think they will change to improve teamwork you're crazy."

You can expect these comments to emerge from the following sources of resistance.

- It's easier to remain as is and to use your comfortable habits.
- Navigating in uncharted waters can be frightening.
- Some personal consequences will occur because everyone will most likely have to change their behaviors to improve working relationships.
- Confusion will enter the change formula when the opposing energy sources begin to clash.
- Some employees will have serious concerns about whether implementing a systematic, data-based process to improve teamwork is really best for the organization at this time.

Figure 2

Energy for Change, Frustration Stage

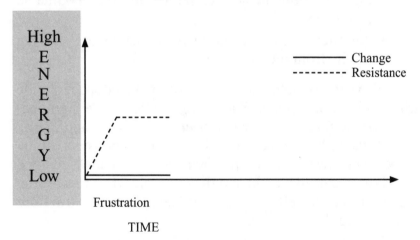

Managing Resistance

Expect resistance. The important point is to expect resistance, so prepare for it. Remember that resistance has two faces. You can consider it as an enemy or as a healthy sign that people are experiencing change. Instead of resisting resistance, embrace it and work with it.

Remaining as is . . . is no option. The antidote to a premature death is making the decision that today's as-is teamwork environment is no longer good enough. Improving working relationships is no longer an option; it *must* happen.

Some of the reasons dictating the need to improve working relationships may sound like:

- "Too many people are looking out for Number One rather than working together to help each other be successful."
- "Territorialism is rampant, and it sabotages cooperation between work units."
- "No one notices if you make an extra effort, so why bother?"
- "Turnover is killing us. We've got to improve working conditions to help us attract and retain valuable employees."
- "Inefficiencies in working relationships are stealing profits from our bottom line."

We've read that the first six feet of a manned space shuttle trip require more energy than the remainder of the flight, because of the force necessary to overcome gravity and inertia and lift the huge weight of the shuttle and its boosters off the launch pad. The process of improving teamwork must contend with both the dead weight and those people who are working against the change effort to keep the teamwork space trip from ever leaving the launch pad.

The burst of energy required to launch the change effort is accomplished by creating an epidemic of frustration. This massive build-up of energy can be created by structuring employee involvement into creating the list of frustrations associated with the as-is teamwork environment. Then make certain that employees know the specific reasons you are engaging in a process to maximize your human capital and working relationships. Remaining as is . . . is not an option.

The 20-60-20 rule. You know that a certain percent of the workforce will resist your team-building efforts from the outset. The more vocal ones will tell you. As you listen to these words, the natural tendency is to become defensive. Rather than being defensive, relax and experience (and enjoy!) the process. Appreciate the fact that the more assertive individuals express resistance openly; some will gripe and groan even more outside your listening distance. Focus your attention to ensure that the resisters and other skeptical employees participate in the change effort. Continue to depend upon the supporters to willingly participate in the performance management system underwriting the change process and to use the behaviors identified in the TeamWork Values Statement.

Communicate. The CEO and other senior leaders discussing the need to improve teamwork can certainly contribute to the strong initial push. As simple as this communication sounds, we cannot overemphasize the importance of this strategy. Their up-front involvement sends a very strong message. All leaders throughout the organization must sing the same tune at every opportunity they have to sing. Fan the fires of frustration to generate the necessary energy to override the initial inertia and neutralize the resistance.

Discuss resistance openly. Demonstrate that it's okay to discuss worries, complaints, and concerns.

- Yes, it is easier to remain as is. But doing what you've always done and expecting a different result is one definition of insanity.
- Yes, the unknown can be frightening. Walking into the unknown can dissipate the fear.
- Yes, everyone will have to improve their interpersonal

performance, and then they will reap the benefits for doing so.

- Yes, there will be confusion, but that can serve as a stimulus for creativity.
- Yes, some employees may question if improving teamwork is the best decision for the organization at this time, and this expression represents concern for their company.

Educate everyone that resistance emerges when individuals do not understand the benefits associated with the change process. Working with resistance represents an opportunity to help resisting individuals to understand the need to change.

Lead by example. In addition to talking about the need to improve teamwork, senior leaders need to participate in writing the TeamWork Values Statement and other preparations required to launch the organizational change effort. The visibility of senior leaders is a critical factor to the success of the cultural change.

Stage Two: Honeymoon

As we mentioned in the discussion about writing the TeamWork Values Statement, to get where you want to go, you must know where you want to be and how to go there. Defining these behavioral templates is the door that must be entered for your company to institutionalize the desired teamwork behaviors.

Upon writing the TeamWork Values Statement, positive energy flows through the halls and drips from the walls. People like what they have seen and heard about the process and the subsequent changes that are certain to follow. People want this teamwork culture today, if not sooner.

Employees' involvement ignites this excitement and creates ownership into the improvement process. Even individuals in the more challenging organizations become excited about the possibility of the TeamWork Values Statement working for them. One organization in particular had amazing seniority—most of the managers had been in their positions for twenty and twenty-five years. The sales manager had the reputation of eating production managers for lunch. He was dreaded and avoided.

We were greeted with the attitude, "I dare you try to change us. We've seen consultants come and go in this organization, and we will see you go as well." The predominant management style was the "do as I tell you" variety. Intimidation and threat were the unwritten rules for achieving what you wanted. The predominant thought was that the intimidating management practices ruts had become graves. In spite of this prevailing attitude, initial excitement was generated through writing this statement, which created the hope that teamwork would be finally improved.

Locking on to the vision created by the TeamWork Values Statement directs the energy generated from the fires of frustration. That is, imagine the frustration (or panic) that would occur if you were in a room that began filling with smoke and you did not know the location of the exits. You would try to create one.

Contrast the image of not finding the exits to one in which the exits in the smoke-filled room are clearly marked. Yes, there is a burst of energy to leave the room, which is done through the exits. Defining the TeamWork Values Statement provides clear direction and the promise to tame the fires of frustrations in the working relationships.

As illustrated in Figure 3, two energy sources propel change: the identified frustration that is pushing the change and the magnetic pull of the desired teamwork culture described in the TeamWork Values Statement.

Figure 3

The Honeymoon

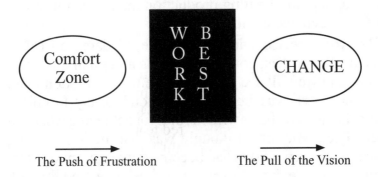

The Push of Frustration   The Pull of the Vision

Resistance

With these two energy sources operating at full throttle, the energy for change skyrockets upward while resistance markedly diminishes, as depicted in Figure 4. The primary sources of resistance operating in this phase are the ease of remaining in the comfort zone and the lingering expression that teamwork does not need to be improved.

Figure 4

Energy for Change, Honeymoon Stage

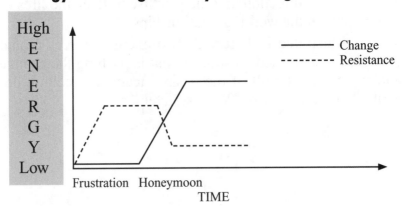

Managing Resistance

Lock onto the vision. The excitement created by writing the values statement and the promise of improved working relationships thrust the change effort forward.

Communicate. The CEO's and other senior leaders' continued involvement in staff meetings throughout the company to spread the gospel of "creating the new tomorrow today" is important. Communicate the word of the new tomorrow through official company publications. Informally talk about the new culture at every opportunity. Review the benefits associated with achieving the desired teamwork culture. The objective is to create a very powerful force that pulls the organization out of its ruts, so *fan the fires of excitement.*

Lead by example. As we've discussed, everyone looks up to watch the leader to see if the words in the values statement are only words, or if they really serve as behavioral guides. You also know that behaviors always speak louder than words, which goes to the issue of every leader converting the words contained within the TeamWork Values Statement into behaviors and leading the implementation of the performance system. Every leader needs to talk the talk *and* walk the walk. Seeing leader participation is believing.

Define and implement teamwork strategies. Put your data to work. Define and implement behavioral solutions that improve interpersonal effectiveness and associated working relationships.

Measure to see success. Demonstrations and evidence of success quiet the soothsayers. Measuring behavior change allows you to see the change. Publish the success that senior-level teams achieve. This top-down change spreads the enthusiasm for change throughout the organization to ensure the integration of the new culture and the measurement process as opposed to merely complying with the new culture.

Stage Three: Pessimism

The initial excitement runs headfirst into the pain associated with change—for example, the time and work required to enter and work with the data, implement the strategies, and the focused effort to change behavior. This pessimism assumes many different voices or masks, but the message is usually the same: Change is too hard, let's stop! You'll hear comments like

- "Maybe we can't do this after all."
- "This improving relationships stuff can be hard on the ego."
- "This whole thing is taking more time than I thought it would."
- "We don't have time for this 'people side' stuff when operational alligators are biting all around."
- "The way things were wasn't so bad. Maybe we should just quit."

The two energy sources encouraging the change effort have lost some of their intensity, as reflected by dashed-lined arrows in Figure 5, and two energy sources encouraging quitting have emerged rather strongly. The latter are created by (1) the discomfort associated with continuing—uncertainty about being successful, the hard work, the time involved, and people's continued resistance—and (2) the lure of the comfort zone's status quo. The results of these pushes and pulls are unease and confusion. The natural tendency to avoid pain and to approach comfort makes it tempting to abandon the change process and return to the security of the comfort zone. These dynamics are illustrated in Figure 5.

Figure 5

Pessimism

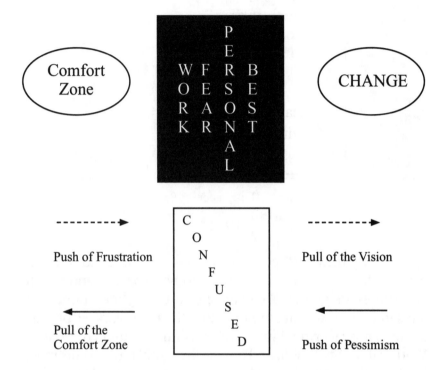

| | Push of Frustration | | Pull of the Vision |
| | Pull of the Comfort Zone | | Push of Pessimism |

Resistance

As depicted in Figure 6, the energy for change plummets while resistance skyrockets during this stage. Some team members are concerned about the lack of progress achieved; enthusiasm gives way to apathy, and morale may appear to be at an all-time low. The hardcore resisters mutter, "We told you so, it's not gonna work." The wait-and-see group may be tempted to agree with them, and even the change agents may have their doubts.

Resistance is now gushing from each of the five sources.

Figure 6

Energy for Change, Pessimism Stage

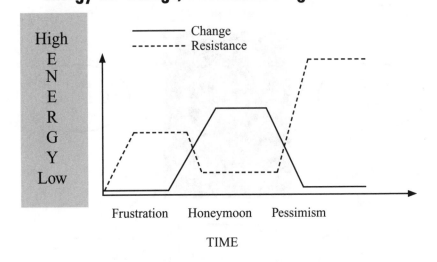

During these difficult times, it is a challenge to remember that this surge of resistance is to be expected and that it constitutes a sign that the change effort is right on target. At the same time, we must realize that the teamwork effort has come to a very critical juncture. Pessimism batters the Team-Work Values Statement and erodes the motivation to continue. Because the pain of continuing appears to be greater and the benefits fewer, the consequences of quitting and declaring this exercise as just another entrant into the idea-of-the-month cemetery can be very tempting. Remember, that is precisely what 70 percent of the organizations that attempt to implement major change efforts do: They quit, because people stop using the systems driving change.

In reality, the senior managers have practiced the process to implement teamwork, but the process is not institutionalized. Up to this point, measuring teamwork has been a rather novel and unique idea. It's been fun to use the data to define and implement teamwork solutions. The momentum obtained during the first two stages of change leads to artificial confidence: "This is easy."

Proactive leadership is crucial at this very critical time to neutralize resistance. When resistance shouts from every source, remember that its expression signals change. Resistance is a teacher and part of the process, rather than being its mortal enemy.

Managing Resistance

Lock on to your TeamWork Values Statement. This statement represents a primary energy source to pull you through these rather trying and difficult times. Recapture some of the initial excitement by loudly and publicly reviewing the benefits associated with the corporate culture of teamwork:

- Better working relationships within work units, between work units, and between work unit leaders and their employees.
- Higher performance and profitability.
- A work environment that inspires commitment, loyalty, and each employee's best effort.
- Job satisfaction and personal growth and development.
- More fun and freedom in the workplace; less anxiety, boredom, and frustration.

Let everyone know that, without a doubt, this culture will be institutionalized within your company.

Staying as is . . . is no option. Coupled with your review of the vision, remind everyone about the frustrations associated with the status quo. To rekindle the epidemic of frustration, review the list of reasons demanding improved teamwork that were written during the initial phases of the process. Make the point that the organization cannot go back to its old ways of doing things, because they weren't working. Implementing the TeamWork Values Statement is the only viable alternative.

Lead by example. This period is an absolutely crucial time for everyone to *see* senior leader's commitment and involvement by using the data and implementing solutions to improve both their work unit's performance as well as their own personal performance. Every member of the management structure must be on board, talking the talk and walking the walk.

People notice positive change. A case in point is the intense production leader's behavior, characterized by "my way" thinking, taking credit when credit was due elsewhere, and getting overly excited and jumping into people's faces while trying to conduct simultaneous conversations.

Then came the big change. He openly discussed the behaviors that were interfering with his personal effectiveness. He started listening and conducting only one conversation at a time. The big surprise was his calm demeanor in situations that previously elicited emotional outbursts. The recognition received for his efforts sent the very important message: teamwork interpersonal skills are important.

When Murphy's Law intrudes, openly discuss frustrations and disappointments. Murphy's Law is alive and well. The success curve is not a straight-line function; things go wrong. Leaders lose their cool and violate the TeamWork Values Statement in word or deed. Teamwork solutions are not implemented as originally agreed. People forget to record their data. The list goes on. You know these occurrences are normal, so remain calm and realize that the lesson being learned is represented in the following formula: disappointment + learning opportunity = organizational intelligence. Continue to exhibit optimism about achieving results while traveling this bumpy road. Perfection is an ideal and Rome wasn't built in a day.

Communicate what has been learned. Publicize what's been learned as the result of Murphy the teacher showing up. This approach helps other individuals and teams deal with similar situations or perhaps avoid them altogether. Psychologically, public acknowledgment of difficulties and solutions accomplishes several other important goals:

- It demonstrates and encourages openness and honesty.
- It reminds everyone of the principle that to err is human and that the point is to learn from one's mistakes.

- It reinforces the perception that, despite setbacks, you're making progress.
- It underlines the organization's continued commitment to change.

Continue to define and implement change strategies. FOCUS serves as an acronym for reminding us to stay on track by keeping the Focus On Change Using Systems. Continue using the teamwork system. Discuss the TeamWork Values Statement and cite examples of it working at every staff meeting; measure behaviors; conduct efficient meetings to review data; and then define, implement, and measure the use of solutions to improve working relationships. Steadfastly using the performance management system builds the foundation for continued success.

Measure success. Seeing and hearing about progress renews the energy for change. Measured progress occurs at two levels: (1) the awareness of engaging the performance management system and (2) the actual data quantifying progress within the people operating systems.

Reward to support the change. Senior leaders continue to play a crucial role when they share their progress, which can take the form of discussing progress during staff meetings throughout the organization, capitalizing on informal conversations, or publishing progress reports in the company's newsletter.

Virtually everyone wants positive recognition for a job well done. Here's an excellent opportunity to spread a few of those "You're doing a good job" words around. Senior leaders need to look for opportunities to recognize the good work of their down-line work units and leaders.

Systematically practicing and encouraging the use of the strategies to convert resistance can help your organization thread its way through the minefields of the pessimism stage. Every ounce of resistance that surfaces provides an opportunity to do something to demonstrate your commitment to make the necessary changes by embodying the values spoken in the TeamWork Values Statement. In fact, resistance gives you the opportunity to show your stuff as a leader, to make resistance your partner in the dance of change.

Stage Four: Optimism

Progress is being made! People begin to realize the TeamWork Values Statement is for real. The light at the end of the tunnel is not an oncoming train.

As illustrated in Figure 7, the two energy sources that encourage change (frustration with the status quo and the magnetic qualities of the vision) have regained strength while the sources of resistance have diminished (shown with dashed lines).

Figure 7

Optimism

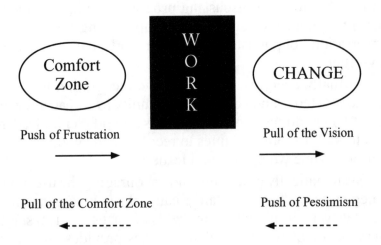

Resistance

Figure 8 illustrates the reversal in the strengths of the energy sources. The improving teamwork path is gaining momentum while much of the resistance has subsided.

Figure 8

Energy for Change, Optimism Stage

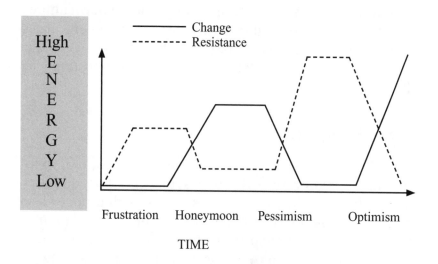

Managing Resistance

Resist the temptation to think you've got it made, because not everyone yet is a believer. Remember that staying in that comfort zone is always easier, so continue emphasizing the systems that have helped you achieve this level of success.

Lock onto your TeamWork Values Statement. Stay focused on the vision. Continue publishing, demonstrating, and talking about the benefits of the teamwork corporate culture. Emphasize that it's not a matter of reaching a single goal but a systematic process of working together. The movement is not over; it's just begun.

Continue implementing change strategies and measure success. People see the numbers and observe the change in atmosphere and behavior. A definite process is in place to convert people problems into behavioral solutions for improvement. Everyone needs to understand that success depends upon their continued efforts.

Keep communicating and rewarding progress. Continue recognizing progress openly and generously.

Lead by example. Do what needs to be done. Continue to do whatever is required to implement the teamwork system: putting the data to work, talking about the new culture, recognizing progress, and ensuring that the communication plan is working. Actions speak louder than words, so be the leader whose behaviors send the message supporting the cultural change.

Stage Five: Success

SUCCESS! Yes, you are now among the elite 30 percent—those organizations that persist in their efforts and successfully manage the dynamics associated with change. The discomfort of the journey was worth it. Your organization is stronger and better equipped to compete in the marketplace, and you and all the employees have attained new knowledge, self-awareness, and skills. Institutionalizing both the structural and behavioral components of your people operating system has expanded your organizational comfort zone as illustrated in Figure 9.

Figure 9

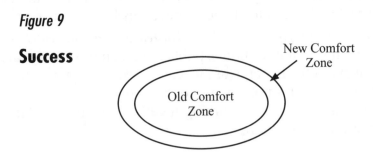

Success

The noise generated by the resistance has all but disappeared, as illustrated in Figure 10.

Figure 10

Energy for Change, Success Stage

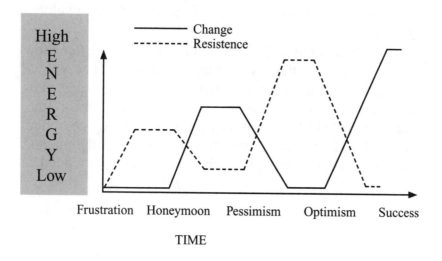

There's a natural tendency to rest on your laurels now that you are achieving what you set out to do. You can take a deep breath, but continue to

- Use the methodologies to track the people numbers and measure success.
- Communicate the institutionalization of your values statement.
- Define and implement solutions for improvement.
- Model and teach the elements of teamwork.
- Lead by example.
- Recognize progress.

Most likely a few hardcore resisters can still be heard to say, "We just got lucky this time," or "It won't last." Consider these comments as a reminder that improving teamwork is an ongoing process and that responding to new events and situations calls for alertness, flexibility, and hard work.

In Closing

Your organization possesses its own dynamic energies. New employees, new technologies, and new projects are being introduced every day. Every day you face new challenges from a fast-paced business climate in an ever-changing global economy.

With this in mind, as we close this chapter we offer a few last comments for the organizational leaders. Once you've institutionalized a teamwork corporate culture, it represents a new comfort zone. Don't let it become too comfortable. Like technical skills, people skills must constantly be honed, improved, and updated. Remember the most carefully planted rose garden soon overgrows with weeds if left unattended.

11 | Accountability and Behavior Change

Accountability is crucial to drive significant behavior change. The focus of this chapter is to show you that accountability is built into the systems approach to improve teamwork.

Implementing People Operating Systems

There is a major difference in the ease of implementing a technical change versus the behavioral changes associated with the TeamWork Values Statement. Technical change uses a template that basically forces people to comply. For example, implementing a computer conversion produces considerable chaos and frustration while people learn the system and work out the wrinkles. But people have to implement the software whether they like it or not—assuming they wish to retain their employment.

The same is true when new equipment is purchased. After the purchase, there is no choice as to whether people are trained on using the equipment. The template for change is there, and people comply.

At the personal level, the TeamWork Values Statement also serves as a template, but it does not force compliance. Each employee has the right to decide the degree to which they integrate the behaviors into their interpersonal interactions. There may not be an "I" in teamwork, but each "I" makes the decision to be an effective team member or not.

We've discussed this dilemma with CEOs who have struggled with implementing people systems. During one such conversation, the CEO explained a new process to integrate the concept of key performance indicators. At defined times, he and his vice presidents meet with division managers to discuss these measurements. When asked why the people data were not part of that conversation, he responded, "That's a good idea. We just never thought about it." It's embarrassing to admit that we had been working with this organization for about a year at this point, and forgetting these data was still easy.

A similar conversation occurred with another CEO who had made tremendous personal improvement moving from being an autocratic, micromanaging CEO to one who empowers staff. On this day, though, he expressed considerable frustration that his down-line managers were not fully utilizing the MBC Software® methodologies and data as a developmental tool. He wanted them to automatically integrate the methodologies into their management systems in the absence of him holding the process accountable.

Three Levels of Accountability

Accountability—doing what is expected to be done—is an essential ingredient to create both personal and organizational change. Unfortunately accountability is not achieved unless someone holds accountable the process of accountability. Because you can only hold accountable what you can see or measure, the emphasis has to be placed on implementing the tangible components of the change system. As you read about the three levels of accountability, think of accountability as a process rather than an event. In other words, it is a management tool that is used every day rather than at specific times or for a given reason. The dilemma when institutionalizing your TeamWork Values Statement is that you can see the value statement, but you can't force anyone to use it.

1. *Organization.* The challenge at the organizational level is to define the expected behaviors. The TeamWork Values Statement and the performance management system comprise the tangible components. As you read the list of desired behaviors, note that each can be readily "seen."

- Defining the TeamWork Values Statement and the behavioral definitions.
- Setting up the measurement system.
  - Training associated with using the MBC Software® and the personal/organizational requirements to successfully improve the teamwork culture.
  - Entering the data.
  - Meeting to put the data to work by reviewing it and defining and measuring the success of solutions to improve people performance within each of the three working relationships inherent in the people operating system.
  - Systematically monitoring the people numbers.
- Implementing the communication plan.
  - Making regularly scheduled updates available so everyone can see the progress achieved.
  - Reviewing the value statement and citing successes at every staff meeting. To some degree, everyone is from Missouri, the Show-Me State. Discussing a value and citing examples of it at work shows everyone the importance of creating the culture defined in the TeamWork Values Statement.
  - Providing recognition for the teamwork improvements.

- Senior organizational leaders attending down-line staff meetings to discuss the progress.
- Incorporating statements from the TeamWork Values Statement into day-to-day operations—for example, "Thank you for volunteering to assist us and helping to create the workplace environment contained in our TeamWork Values Statement."

Now that you can observe each of the above components, you can make certain that people use these tools as part of your system to improve working relationships. You can't dictate the use of the TeamWork Values Statement, but you do have more control to ensure that these tangible components of the performance management system are completed to send the message about the importance of implementing the TeamWork Values Statement. Using the system encourages people to incorporate these behaviors into their day-to-day operations. If you should stop using the performance management system, you can be certain that the behavior will deteriorate and the TeamWork Values Statement will become a memory. We can't overemphasize this point; when you stop using the systems, behavior reverts back to its original state much like a stretched rubber band returns to its normal state upon being released.

2. *Management.* Accountability incorporates two processes for managers. The first is leading by example, or walking the talk. Day-to-day behaviors must mirror your TeamWork Values Statement. Leading by example also includes the systematic utilization of the performance system components listed above. Second is teaching your people to replicate your actions to use the performance system as designed and to walk the talk of the TeamWork Values Statement. As an up-line supervisor, you will not always be present to observe your down-line managers or employees walking the talk of your TeamWork Values Statement, but you can review their data with them on a regular basis to be certain the performance management system is being used as designed.

3. *Self.* All of the employees must hold themselves accountable to do what is expected. This level of accountability is demonstrated by being a willing participant in the change process and improving interpersonal behaviors (here's the "I" in teamwork again). Imagine how much more efficient your people, their working relationships, and your organization would be if every employee simply demonstrated personal accountability.

Seven-Step Personal Change Process Demonstrating Personal Accountability

Personal accountability exhibited to use the management system to institutionalize your TeamWork Values Statement is an exercise of self-discipline and behavioral changes that must be made is dependent upon using a seven-step process. As you read them, note the flow-chart characteristic in that the preceding step must be completed before advancing to the next one. A block at any given step results in truncating the change process.

1. *Recognizing the need to change.* Improving your interpersonal efficiency begins with recognizing the need to do so. The need for change is based on the realization that the disadvantages of the as-is situation outweigh the advantages: "I must change as it is no longer beneficial for me to continue doing what I've been doing." This first step sounds deceivingly simple, but admitting the need to change can be a dent to one's ego; it hurts a little bit to realize that we might not be as good as we would like to think.

Our experience has been that this step frequently represents a major hurdle. For example, a vice president of operations terrified his staff by skewering them whenever a decision was made that he did not consider correct. The end result was that no mistakes were made, because nothing was done until he gave his personal blessing.

When his intimidation was brought to his attention, his response was, "They have nothing to fear from me. You can count on one hand the number of people I've fired." The fear he introduced in the workplace not only stifled creativity and decision making, it also created the unwritten behavioral code to cover your behind.

He did not understand why his team members were intimidated by his emotional outbursts. According to him, it was business as usual and everything was back to normal once the emotional release was made. He did not conceptualize that the sting of a bee is often worse than the physical damage created by the bee's bite.

2. *Accepting responsibility for your behavior.* The current day-to-day operation's rule seems to be to blame someone for our behavior instead of taking responsibility for it. We're reminded of the senior-level manager who believed that because he had always been shy and introverted and failed to hold his staff accountable, he would always be that way. He blamed history for his present behavior. Psychologically he is stuck in a rut that is serving as his grave.

For just a moment, think about your wealth if you received a dollar for every time you said or heard said, "That person really made me mad!" The truth of the matter is that no one causes you to do anything. The action of others influence your thinking, but you have choices and decide how you respond. You see choices being made at work every day. One person goes ballistic when a frustration occurs, while another calmly approaches the situation in an effort to efficiently use the frustrating situation to improve the process.

No one can force you to exercise your option to use the behaviors contained within your TeamWork Values Statement. Your behavior tells those with whom you work about your decision to value this statement. To be a high-performing individual you must accept your responsibility and walk the talk of the statement or walk out of the organization. A chain is only as strong as its weakest length, or to put it another way, it only takes one little wet spot to bend the strongest noodle. You don't want to be the chain's weak length or the noodle's wet spot.

3. *Know the desired behaviors.* To do what needs to be done, you must know what needs to be done. That statement speaks to the heart of the issue of defining the expected behaviors in your TeamWork Values Statement, the components of the performance management system that we detail in this book, and the specific behavioral solutions that you or your work unit can implement to improve interpersonal performance. Any confusion associated with any of these sets of behaviors needs to be clarified immediately so everyone specifically knows the expected behaviors. These defined behaviors constitute the behavioral blueprints, and your responsibility is to put them to work for you.

4. *Willing to change.* The wrench has yet to be invented that can be inserted into someone's head to adjust the "I will change" screws. You still hold the keys to unlock your own door for personal change. Making the decision to change is predicated on the requirement that you recognize the advantages of implementing the behaviors contained in your TeamWork Values Statement compared to not implementing them. That is, your intensity associated with the willingness to change is positively correlated with the size of the gap between the advantages of the new behavior versus the advantages of the as-is behaviors.

Remember purchasing an item that exceeded your budget? The advantages of owning that item were intense, thereby creating a very strong magnetic pull that sucked money out of your pocket. Ideally, the behaviors contained in your TeamWork Values Statement likewise have a strong magnetic pull.

5. *Create a visual image of implementing the desired behaviors.* Your performance is regulated by what you see yourself doing. The importance of this principle is often overlooked when discussing personal change issues, but we only

have to look to the sports world to recognize the importance of this visualization process. Jack Nicklaus is credited for making the statement that he sees a perfect swing and the ball landing exactly where he wants it to before swinging the club. Today, visualization is a standard operating procedure with high-performing athletes.

Bill Russell, the famous Boston Celtics center, even credits his phenomenal career to the visualization process. He was just an ordinary basketball player until he had the opportunity to spend one month working with other gifted athletes. He watched these athletes' every move, and he watched his stellar performance through the personal visions he created.

One of the authors, Larry, did the same. He was a frightened, shy, and terrible instructor the first time he stood before a class of Introductory Psychology students. He was miserable. Ultimately he placed the image of Bernat Herskovets, one of his favorite undergraduate psychology instructors, vividly in his mind; while teaching he *was* Bernat Herskovets. This process reengineered him and was the forerunner to help him become a public speaker.

The bottom line is that if there is even one behavior in your TeamWork Values Statement that you cannot visualize implementing, then it will not become integrated into your behavioral library. We recommend completing a self-assessment exercise with your value statement to determine the degree you see yourself implementing each behavior. That exercise can be as simple as answering yes or no as you examine each behavior, or you can use a Likert Scale to measure the degree you see yourself using each behavior.

To be a high performer and demonstrate personal accountability, work to create your personal image of being the person described in that statement. Enjoy that image and the associated benefits of being an excellent role model and receiving the admiration of those with whom you work. Remember that people care about people who care about them.

6. *Practice.* Up to this point, these steps have been preparation for change. In step six, you are putting forth the

effort to change. Changing occurs at three levels. First, as just described in step five, you can practice within when you're without. You can practice when sitting in your chair by simply turning the switch on in your personal video. You can create any scenario you wish and be as perfect as you want to be.

The second is role-playing. You can create specific workplace scenarios and practice engaging the desired behaviors in the training classroom or with a coworker or friend.

The third is to take advantage of the opportunities to put your TeamWork Values Statement to work every day, all day long in terms of how you work with your fellow employees. Every day is a practice session. You likewise practice change as you

- Discuss your TeamWork Values Statement and ask others at every staff meeting to share a personal story of using the statement.
- Conduct meetings to use the data associated with measuring the people systems.
- Use the phrase daily, "According to our TeamWork Values Statement, we need to do . . ."
- Teach others to use the TeamWork Values Statement.
- Ask others to provide you immediate feedback should they think you are behaving outside of the TeamWork Values Statement.
- Communicate successes in meetings, internal newsletters, corporate videos, and other celebrations.

Seize every opportunity to practice, practice, and practice some more.

7. *Feedback.* Feedback can occur at three levels. First is to pat yourself on the back for implementing your TeamWork Values Statement and the performance system to drive change. Celebrate your personal successes. While celebrating personal successes, continue to monitor your behavior and make the necessary adjustments to increase your performance.

The second is recognizing success through the data.

One of the advantages associated with using an electronic performance system such as the MBC Software® is the immediate feedback crucial for behavior change. For example, we worked with a challenging senior manager who initially thought he was nearly perfect. If you didn't think so, all you had to do was ask him. Only through the use of data did he recognize the need to change and eventually implement several behavioral strategies to improve his interpersonal performance. The improvement prevented him from the need to find other employment!

The third level is providing each other with immediate feedback. Obviously you want to create the psychological environment that your coworkers can spontaneously provide you both positive recognition for your efforts to improve working relationships and constructive feedback when your behavior had an adverse impact. You are in a very powerful and effective position when your coworkers feel free to offer you this feedback. The ultimate level of emotional maturity for a work unit occurs when each member can both give and receive this level of feedback.

The importance of immediate feedback can be illustrated by the process of teaching a blindfolded marksman to hit the target. Blindfold the marksman, turn him around a couple of times, and ask him to hit the target? The likelihood of success is not great. But provide immediate and specific feedback to the marksman, and he can quickly adjust to hit the target. Any delay in that feedback increases the difficulty associated with hitting the target. The psychological bottom line is that immediate feedback is crucial for behavior change.

In Closing

Just imagine the exciting workplace that would be created if all employees would hold themselves accountable to use the behaviors contained within their TeamWork Values Statement. When holding yourself accountable, you are likewise being accountable to your coworkers and the organization as a whole. Personal accountability is a key to organizational change.

Part Four
PERSONAL
DEVELOPMENT

12 | Living in a Fishbowl

The amount of influence a given individual exerts upon the corporate culture is positively correlated with that person's level of authority in the organization, with the CEO obviously having the most influence. Organizational leaders must recognize their impact upon the organization. These individuals are in the fishbowl, and employees act like cats watching their every move while swimming in the fishbowl.

Knowing behavior sends such a message is the reason that Herb Kelleher schedules time to work the front line with other employees. He wants to send the message that customer service drives the success of Southwest Airlines.

It's the same reason that Sam Walton visited his Wal-Mart stores to talk to associates and customers. Walton wanted associates to feel special and important to the success of the Wal-Mart story.

Bob Lutz, former vice chairman of Chrysler who is credited for turning Chrysler around for the second time, understood the impact of the CEO's behavior. He routinely spent time talking to Chrysler employees. According to Lutz, "The best leaders are usually humble, which comes from a self-confidence." He discussed the fact that some CEO's big ego sends fear throughout the organization that breeds the cover-your-behind mentality. This fear can ruin an organization, according to Lutz.

The CEO of the organization is in a special category for at least two reasons. First is the magnitude of his or her impact upon the organization. Second, the CEO's behavior can be just as damaging to the corporate culture as it can be positive.

A financial holding company considered improving its customer service culture to both invert its traditional organizational pyramid to "move decision making closer to the customer" and to identify more opportunities to "wrap their services around" that customer. After completing a diagnostic process to learn more about the organization's corporate culture, a meeting was scheduled with the CEO and the committee responsible to oversee the process to improve customer service practices, to discuss the observations.

The first observation shared was that employees had consistently expressed that senior managers were not friendly. The question was raised about how employees could be friendly with customers if senior managers were not friendly with their own employees. The CEO quickly responded, "It's true. I often walk through the company without speaking to employees. But that's not going to change."

The second observation was that the decision-making process appeared to be very slow and was tightly controlled by senior managers. The inconsistency between being autocratic on the one hand, while trying to empower employees to make customer service decisions on the other was discussed with the committee. The CEO again commented, "The employees are again correct. Decision making is tightly controlled, and that won't change either."

How can you attempt to empower employees and create a friendly, external customer service environment when the internal customer service environment is cold and autocratic? These styles are mutually exclusive. In this case, the CEO's own social style doomed his organization's efforts to change.

The clear choice was to recommend that his company's conversations about "improving their customer service culture" go no further than this discussion.

Another CEO is a nice guy. He wanted his staff to do what they knew needed to be done, because they like the working relationship with him. Accountability and meeting time frames were foreign words in their culture. The unwritten rule was that it's no big deal to not do what has been agreed to. If there are any consequences, there are a few unpleasant words, promises to do better, and then a return to business as usual.

The entire organization is a victim of this leadership style. Every department—safety, quality, maintenance, and production—struggled to get what is needed from other departments. The rule to entice cooperation was, "You do me a favor and I'll return it."

Smaller incidents can be equally revealing. Returning from lunch with the president and several vice presidents of another company, notice was made that someone had strewn paper at the front door to their corporate offices. The suggestion was made to clean it up. The company's president looked at the trash and said without hesitation, "We have maintenance people who will do that!"

Back in the privacy of his office, the president was told he'd just earned an "F" on his leadership report card. He was surprised by the grade, but then understood that he had missed an excellent opportunity to demonstrate that he will perform whatever task is necessary to get the job done. Instead he had, in effect, just told his vice presidents that whenever they see something that needs to be done, they should automatically assign the task to someone else. Upon leaving the building three hours later, a maintenance worker was cleaning the mess. So for three hours, trash greeted the company's customers!

While telling this story to a group of executives at another company, the marketing director suddenly excused himself from the meeting. When he returned I inquired about his absence. He said, "There's been a child's shoe lying in our flower box for the past week. I decided I needed to go throw it away."

Fish Rot from the Head Down

The comfort zone is the problem. We tend to do what is comfortable rather than doing what needs to be done. For example, a company's management sought to create a teamwork environment within its manufacturing facility. As the effort began in earnest, on-line employees talked about the importance of seeing the general manager on the production floor (many of them claimed they wouldn't even recognize the man).

Although he paid lip service to his company's new teamwork culture, the general manager never took the opportunity to demonstrate his own commitment to teamwork by using a walking-around style of management. Requests from his staff to do so fell on deaf ears. He stayed off the floor. Eventually other staff began to complain about completing "useless assignments" to improve working relationships. The end result: no changes.

To cite another example, a company completed a training program to create a new sales culture. In addition to the program costs, employees spent many hours each week in the classroom for a period of about six months; with staff time included, the total cost was hundreds of thousands of dollars.

There was never a return on the investment because the CEO's reputation for "chasing rabbits" sabotaged the training program. Upon completing the training program the CEO jumped to another idea. So the sales training program died in the classroom, and the course manuals ended up gathering dust on the bookshelves.

In another instance the CEO admitted to being overcontrolling because he didn't trust lower-level managers to make decisions, but he thought he could change. The accounting department determined that about 70 percent of purchase orders were for expenditures for less than two hundred dollars. The standard operating procedure required every requisition to be approved by every up-line supervisor, including the CEO. The accounting personnel recommended that each manager be given the authority to spend up to two hundred dollars without further approval, to save the cost of pushing paper from one desk to another. The table veto was the fate of this recommendation. In the end, a micromanaging CEO killed yet another change effort.

Note that in each of the preceding examples, the willingness on the part of the senior manager to change just a little could have had a tremendously positive impact upon the working relationship and possibly major change efforts on the part of the organization.

Senior manager behaviors can send shock waves throughout an organization, but behavioral impacts do not start and end with the CEO. The personalities of other managers also have an impact.

This first-line supervisor described himself as a logical problem solver who encouraged employee input and team-based decisions. The members of his so-called team presented a different view. They described him as being a dictatorial and demanding writer of arbitrary rules, and explosive to the point of seeming to enjoy the opportunity to scold an employee in front of his or her peers. A department that had once been characterized by high morale, productivity, and profitability quickly became one of griping, moaning, and red ink. The situation had deteriorated to the point that employees were threatening to walk off the floor.

Another first-line supervisor was one of those about whom his people said, "You have to see what kind of mood he's in before you talk to him." On good days, everything was usually okay. But on bad days everyone avoided contact with the man, and the staff felt jumpy, waiting for an explosion. To make matters worse, this supervisor constantly complained about other departments. No one cooperated, according to him; he was the diamond in a field of stones. Actually, he was more like an island that no one wanted to visit.

Our last example is the purchasing manager who loudly and constantly complained about other departments not completing purchase orders completely or accurately. According to him, his department was flooded with work that was supposed to be completed by the person submitting the purchase order.

Would the purchasing manager work to ensure that people knew how to fill out purchase orders accurately and completely? No. Did people in other departments want to cooperate with him or his department? No. You know that the purchasing department touches the lives of every employee in an organization, so you can imagine the havoc that this one individual created.

You've seen these situations and more before, and you know the rest of the story; low morale, lack of cooperation, and low levels of production or poor delivery of services are the results. These thieves steal money from the financial bottom line, and the irony is that this financial loss is created while at the same time organizational leaders are working hard to maximize profits. Yes, fish rot from the head down, and it costs the organization money.

Sticking Out Like a Sore Thumb

As we wrote this chapter, we were struck that there seem to be more examples of leadership behaviors having an adverse impact upon working relationships than positive impacts, which leads us to ask the following question. Does the number of leaders who demonstrate behaviors that have a negative impact outnumber those who have a positive impact upon the working relationship, or are these behaviors just noticed and discussed more?

Before we answer this question, the work of Jim Collins, as reported in his best-selling book *Good to Great,* relates to this issue. Collins conducted research to learn the leadership characteristics of individuals who led their company from good to great status. His research team reviewed the companies that appeared in the *Fortune* 500 from 1965 to 1995 and identified only eleven companies that matched their criteria.

In reality, several factors affect the answer to the question about the number of leaders who have a negative or positive impact. First, there is the tendency to remember the negative events and forget positive ones. Second, research concludes that we spend up to 80 percent of our waking hours thinking negative thoughts. That in itself is depressing, would you agree? But look at the host of variables that illustrate our propensity to be negative.

- Do negative rumors spread more quickly in your organization than positive ones or vice versa?
- What do you discuss more frequently in your organization, what people are doing right or what they are doing wrong?
- Emphasis is placed on what is wrong rather than what is right in the search to improve both personal and organizational performance.
- When are you most likely to notice an employee's behavior, when they do something good or make a mistake?
- Do you listen to news or read newspapers to learn what is going right in this world, or to learn about wars and the number of people murdered?

Or third, perhaps the root cause of all the noise associated with leadership behaviors that negatively impact working relationships is attributed to the lack of systems to define and teach the behaviors that create positive working relationships within the people operating systems.

The ironic fact is that we want to be happy individuals. Howard Cutler, M.D., wrote the book *The Art of Happiness* based on his interviews with the Holiness Dalai Lama. The position of that book is that happiness is one of the universal purposes of being a human. We want positive events to dominate our lives. How can that happen when we spend so much time thinking about the negative?

In Closing

The bottom line is that leaders are in the organizational fishbowl, and their behaviors have a tremendous impact upon the organization. Everything they say, don't say, do, and don't do sends a message. Perhaps Gandhi's quote, "Be the change you want to see in this world," summarizes the essence of this chapter. Leaders' greatest challenge may be to model the change they wish to see in their organizations.

13 | **Will the Real Me Please Stand Up?**

Excuse the negative description of a positive event, but a recent advertisement tagline read, "You won't get very far if you don't get along with others," which speaks to the heart of the matter and the importance of interacting with other people. You must be the person that others like.

First, being liked is essential for you to maximize your personal influence. Other employees will enjoy being around you, will be more likely to listen to you, and will be more cooperative and willing to help you succeed.

Second, being liked by your up-line supervisor(s) increases the likelihood you will be given additional opportunities to demonstrate your competencies.

Third, being liked helps create the psychological environment that stimulates creativity, high performance, and increased profits within your work group.

Fourth, your interpersonal behaviors are part of your personal marketing package and can increase your value to the organization and increase the probability of promotion and other career advancement opportunities.

Fifth, being liked increases your effectiveness as a role model to lead change efforts, including the team-building system detailed in this book.

Sixth, it is the right thing to do.

Now we challenge you to generate a list of meaningful benefits for being the person no one likes.

To maximize your interpersonal performance and working relationships, consider Laurie Beth Jones's opening line to her best-selling book, *Jesus, CEO:* "Leaders know who they are." You must know which of your behaviors have a positive impact as well as those that have a negative one.

Without delving too much into psychology, let's consider the complexity of interpersonal performance in organizations. Your behavior and that of your coworkers is the product of a combination of several psychological variables.

1. *Personality.* Your behaviors are the result of interactions between your genetic composition and your learning history. No one knows for certain how much either contributes to the behaviors that others see you exhibit. It is generally believed that the basic foundation for your behaviors is finalized by your sixth birthday. If that is true, then a great deal of learning occurred at a time when you did not have the opportunity to apply much logic to your foundation. Obviously, at that time of your life, you had no chance to know the behaviors that would be important for your professional career. The end result is a workforce complicated by diversity and uniqueness.

2. *Self-confidence and self-esteem.* Although each of us is a product of several psychological variables, we highlight self-confidence and self-esteem, because they are such significant contributors to our emotional health and the behaviors we exhibit. Think of self-confidence as expressed in the "I can" attitude. In other words, self-confidence is exhibited in knowing what you can do. Self-esteem, on the other hand, represents the degree to which "I like myself." You can be self-confident and still suffer from a loss of self-esteem. Con-

versely, you can have a positive self-esteem without being confident to successfully complete some behaviors. These two variables touch lives in numerous ways. For example, the insecurity inherent in a lack of self-confidence may be seen in the work environment as the "I know everything" mask that some people hide behind. Another individual may lock herself into her comfort zone and be afraid to even peek at an opportunity to step out of it. When you consider the fact that every one of your colleagues' behavior represents an attempt to work with these issues along with other psychological factors, the complexity of the work environment becomes extremely interesting.

3. *Unconscious.* There is a stranger living within each of us. That is, information contained in our unconscious mind remains unavailable to us, but at the same time impacts our behaviors.

The combination of psychological variables contributes to the behavioral uniqueness that you and your coworkers demonstrate. You already know the impact this diversity can create in the workplace, and the challenge is to harness this uniqueness into a high-performing people operating system. To do so, you and other employees are asked to modify your behaviors to align your personal resources with your TeamWork Values Statement and to maximize interpersonal performance. Doing so requires knowing who you are, which represents another challenge.

Will Your Achilles' Heel Please Stand Up?

The story is told about the mother who held her son's heels and dipped him into the river Styx to ensure that he grew to be an invulnerable warrior, and he grew to be a great warrior, until an arrow pierced his heel, resulting in his death. His mother failed to realize that where she held onto him remained dry while being dipped into the river. The story has since become known as the Achilles Syndrome, referring to the fact that all of us participate in behaviors that weaken our working relationships.

Knowing your Achilles' heel means knowing what you do that interferes with, adversely impacts, or even destroys your working relationships. Two very important variables complicate this quest for self-knowledge, however. First is that you don't see yourself as others do; therefore, you may not know the specific behaviors that have an adverse impact upon others. Second, knowing your behavioral strengths and weaknesses is more of a challenge than looking into the mirror to see what you do or do not like about your physical appearance. Unfortunately, we can be blinded and not see the behaviors that adversely impact our working relationships and our career. Speaking of physical characteristics, millions of dollars are spent each year to transform the characteristics that serve as the physical Achilles' heels into works of artistic beauty. We wish it would be that easy to transform the behavioral Achilles' heels. Each of us has to serve as our own plastic surgeon as we struggle to transform our behaviors into a work of art.

Take John into consideration. John is a production supervisor saturated with his own ego. His way is the only way. Correcting his people's mistakes consists of dictatorial orders with all the emotional trimmings. Production workers intensely dislike him. They are extremely fearful and defensive whenever he appears in the work area.

Worse is that John did not believe those who brought his disruptive behaviors to his attention. John could not see his behaviors causing these adverse reactions in others. John, like anyone else, cannot manage what he cannot see. Employees began a campaign to have him removed from the company. In the end he did leave, to the joyous celebration of those left behind.

Mary has the reputation of getting even. If she does not like you or thought you were challenging her authority, you quickly became a memory in that organization. She was a feared lady. But when questioned about this, she did not accept that reputation. In her eyes she merely terminated people who were not doing their job. Mary was unaware of the impact of her behavior and the fact that she was intensely disliked.

Most organizations have a John or a Mary who is in the process of seriously impacting working relationships and careers. In essence, such individuals are victims of their own blind spot.

Companies work hard to not be a victim of not knowing. For example, consider safety. Companies complete strenuous product testing to ensure product safety. The company's very existence could be wiped out if their product causes consumer harm.

Think of the blind spot as part of our psychological immunity system that operates in a manner similar to the physical one. That is, whenever our physical immunity system detects a foreign and potentially dangerous substance that has entered the body, it works to keep the body healthy by ridding itself of the foreign entity. The psychological immunity system also works to keep us healthy. Our psychological environment contains information that would be painful if we became conscious of it. To prevent ourselves from self-inflicted pain, the immunity system keeps it from our conscious mind. If we can't see it, it must not exist. If it does not exist, it cannot hurt us. To be maximally effective, we must find a way to override this immunity system to learn about the content that can adversely impact our personal performance by sabotaging our interpersonal effectiveness.

Reduce the Size of Your Emotional Blind Spot

We have five windows through which we can look to learn more about ourselves and to develop a high level of self-awareness and thereby reduce our blind spot. The five windows are listed below.

1. Thoughts
2. Feelings
3. Behaviors
4. Asking Others
5. Self-Assessment Techniques

Only through knowing the truth can you gain your freedom from the Achilles' heel and your blind spot. Once you learn that you are not perfect (which is okay), and that you engage behaviors that adversely impact the working relationship, you are then in a position to reduce the size of your emotional blind spot and work to improve your behavior. The key that will allow you to see the truth is your willingness to accept the pain of the truth. Whatever you learn about yourself is okay. It is you, so it should be okay.

As Pogo once said, "We have met the enemy, and he is us." Pogo's statement also means, "To be part of the solution, I must realize that I am part of the problem." Now let's turn our attention to examining the five windows.

Thoughts, Feelings, and Behavior. These first three windows are obviously the most important because they are our constant companions. They continually provide information about ourselves, if we are willing to see. To do this, it is important to ask, "Why do I think, feel, or act this way?"

As you begin examining your personal data, you will find another interesting phenomenon. Situations that are associated with the most uncomfortable thoughts, feelings, and behaviors provide the richest opportunities for learning. We must also admit that taking advantage of these learning opportunities is difficult. First, we naturally tend to avoid what is uncomfortable, but obviously we cannot learn through avoiding. Second, when we are experiencing such instances in real time, our awareness is focused on the heat of the moment and away from examining our thoughts, feelings, and behaviors. When that happens, take time after the incident to examine your thoughts, feelings, and actions.

When asking yourself why you feel or act as you do, you may find that your first reaction is, "I don't know." Nevertheless, continue asking the question anyway. Periodically think about the situation and your different reactions. When the student is ready, the answer appears.

Consider the example of Ron, a young administrator who became extremely defensive whenever a staff member questioned one of his decisions. His first response was to offer arguments in defense of his decision with an accompanying feeling level consumed with fear and much uncertainty. When Ron examined his responses, he concluded that his insecurity stemmed from a strong fear of failing and a lack of self-confidence. His defensive behavior pattern was a feeble attempt to mask these feelings. Realizing this insecurity helped him be more willing to accept feeling threatened and to recognize it as an opportunity to use the specialized knowledge of others.

Understanding the dynamics underlying destructive behaviors provides an excellent stepping-stone to begin using more effective behaviors. Like Ron, accepting the pain of the truth opens the door for self-improvement. Harold Bloomfield, M.D., provided an excellent exercise to help learn about your Achilles' heels in his book *Achilles Syndrome*. Bloomfield asks the reader to complete a series of "except-for" and "if-only" statements. Identify your emotional struggle and place it in a sentence, "I would be more _____ , if only. . . ." Complete that sentence at least ten times. We know that the first five answers are superficial ones, but the last five most likely contain valuable information for you to glean insights about your behavior. We used this format and generated the following statements to illustrate the exercise. Please use these or write more personal ones for you. The important point is to put the exercise to work for you.

Will Your Real Achilles' Heel Please Stand Up?

1. I would feel better about myself if only. . . .
2. I would be more successful as a leader if only. . . .

3. I would feel that my life had more meaning and purpose if only. . . .
4. I would be able to work more cooperatively with others if only. . . .
5. I would be better at defining my vision or goals for my company if only. . . .
6. I would have more self-confidence if only. . . .
7. I would be more effective at communicating my goals if only. . . .
8. I would be more effective at encouraging cooperation if only. . . .
9. I would be more effective at recognizing high performance if only. . . .
10. I would be more effective at developing trust if only. . . .
11. I would be more effective at empowering others if only. . . .
12. I would achieve more of my goals if only. . . .
13. I would be more effective at helping my staff grow if only. . . .
14. I could get staff more involved in decision making if only. . . .

Asking Others. Another component of the process to learn about yourself is becoming aware of the impact your behaviors have on others. Because you don't see yourself as others do, your self-examination may not provide all the information you need. Using the fourth window or asking others for feedback can help you see the perception you have created in the eyes of others.

This window poses more of a challenge than found in the first three windows, because of your ego involvement and learning the inconsistencies between the perception others have about you versus your self-perception. In reality, the perception that others have about you can be more important than your self-perception in terms of your ultimate success in the organization.

Using the measurement methodologies introduced in this book to ask others to quantify their perceptions about your behavior is certainly putting yourself at risk to learn the degree that your self-perception matches that held by others. Yet seeing yourself as others see you is precisely the information that can be most valuable to you. It's nice to learn about everything you are doing well. That information boosts your ego, inflates your hat size, and basically makes you feel like a winner. Feeling like a winner is important for your psychological well-being. You also need to identify the gaps created by believing your behavior is at a higher level than that perceived by others. Such information is most valuable when used to help you see your blind spots.

We don't want to leave this section with the thought that using numbers is the only way to obtain feedback from others. There is still the good old-fashioned way: Ask others for their feedback. Each of us could benefit from a coach, mentor, or trusted friend who can provide feedback to help us improve our interpersonal performance.

There is a trick when asking others for feedback that can soften the impact and make it easier for the individual to provide feedback. Note the following question speaks to improvement, "What do you think I can do to improve?" This question provides a guideline for the answer to be more positive and emotionally acceptable while at the same time providing information that you need to know. Contrast the first question for improvement with "What did you think about how I . . . ?" This question opens the door for the feedback to be anything from flattery to destructive criticism. You don't want that. Chances are that the other person won't like it either. So ask for information that can be useful and more palatable for everyone concerned.

Supervisors should continuously monitor their working relationships with their employees, peer group, and their up-line supervisor. These supervisors can ask, "What can I do to help you to be more successful?" Asking this question is an excellent procedure to assess the degree to which others feel free to offer such suggestions. Ultimately, the degree of openness to contribute valuable information is determined by how the supervisor listens to understand and then uses that information for personal improvement.

Self-Assessment Techniques. The fifth window to look through to increase self-knowledge is the use of self-assessment techniques. These techniques are designed to assess your perception of your behavior, according to some dimension at the point in time when you complete the assessment. These techniques are designed to provide a mirror to help you see yourself as others may see you. Three major advantages in using self-assessment techniques are as follows.

1. You can take them in the privacy of your office or home.

2. The information provided by the self-assessment can provide valuable guidance to improve your interpersonal performance.

3. As you understand yourself better, you will likewise learn about others.

The validity of self-assessment techniques depends upon the honesty of your self-evaluation. You can answer the questions as you desire. For example, you could answer questions while imagining yourself to be the person you would like to be. Or you could answer as you think you really are. You could even answer questions as you imagine a friend or spouse would answer them. But remember: garbage in, garbage out. Honest data is the only way this exercise can benefit your self-improvement efforts.

Numerous self-assessment techniques are available. We're sure your human resources people can assist you; if not, please contact us.

Another approach is to create a self-assessment technique with your TeamWork Values Statement. Doing so can be as simple as using a Likert Scale to measure the frequency with which you use the behaviors in your day-to-day interactions with your coworkers.

Putting Your Self-Knowledge to Work

Becoming more aware of yourself, however, is no guarantee that you will do anything with this information. Because you are in control, you decide what to do with your new awareness. You have the following three options:

1. Deny the information or resist the truth (e.g., "This just is not me").
2. Accept the information as having some validity but avoid doing anything by ignoring what you learn.
3. Accept the information as true and use it for self-improvement. In other words, the information you learn from one or more of these five windows can help you recognize the need to change or complete Step 1 in the seven-step process for personal change.

The first two options produce the same end result: Nothing constructive is done. Either of these decisions may lead to professional suicide, and the message sent to your colleagues is that self-improvement is not important. We've discussed several examples in which individuals were not able to see themselves as others did and denied the information. In some respects the destruction that can occur from the second option or with one's full knowledge and consent may be even more disturbing than not being able to see the destruction based on one's emotional blind spot. We are referring to individuals who make a conscious decision to continue to use damaging behaviors in spite of the adverse effects. For example, Debbie is all-knowing. She constantly tells everyone who will listen about how important she is by acting like an encyclopedia, and she quickly lets you know about her knowledge. Here is another person who is avoided like a disease.

Debbie is aware of the words she uses. She recognizes how such behaviors impact personal relationships. Her rationalization is that coworkers need to accept her as the person she is.

Hence, the first two options are really not options for you, if you want to be maximally effective.

In Closing

One more issue deserves attention before closing this chapter. You are very likely involved in a process of continual improvement of the product(s) or service(s) that your company provides. To do that, you use a system to accomplish this objective. As you know, your business must continually improve, or one day you may not be in business. In this chapter we have detailed a system for continued self-discovery. In essence, you can use this self-discovery system to increase your personal-product knowledge. Just as it is true that only through product knowledge are you able to fully utilize the business resources available to you, *also only through knowing yourself are you able to fully utilize your valuable personal resources*.

Consider yourself as if you were a small business. As an individual, you are selling your knowledge and skills to the company. As you know, in order for your company to remain competitive and to succeed, it must be on the cutting edge of change to innovatively meet the needs of your customers. As a small business, you need to remain competitive, and you succeed by being on the cutting edge of change to innovatively meet the needs of your most important customer: the company you work for. Everything you do to improve your self-worth and value to your company serves to write your personal guarantee for success.

Part Five
LEADING
YOU INTO
TOMORRROW

14 | People Systems Taking You into the Future

As long as there are organizations, people will need to work together. That has been true since early man banded together to conduct the necessary activities to ensure their survival, and nothing in the foreseeable future will change this basic tenet. Even though evolution has brought forth many changes as society progressed through the agricultural and industrial ages to reach the current information age and into the people age, the need for people working together in a cooperative manner has been constant.

People Systems Pave the Road into the Future

Putting on our psychic glasses to look into the future, we see a continuing need for the people operating system in the ever-changing work environment. As long as people are required to cooperate, they need a blueprint outlining the expected behaviors to ensure this cooperation. A host of extraneous variables are at work to destroy high-performing working relationships, and a systematic process to continually improve teamwork can prevent these destructive forces from taking their toll.

"The devil made me do it." In the words of Harold Kushner's best-selling book, *Bad Things Happen to Good People.* Good people are going to engage in behaviors that interrupt working relationships for whatever reasons. People are dynamic energy systems, and the variability created by people produces working relationships that are likewise dynamic energy systems. Perhaps gene manipulation will someday allow for the creation of the perfect worker, that is, one in whom the ideal teamwork behaviors are genetically determined, thereby eliminating the impact of freedom of choice in the workplace. Until that happens, our guess is that freedom of choice will continue requiring the need for a set of behavioral blueprints.

Changing Work Environment. People are constantly cycling through the organization. Current workers become a memory, and new personalities need to be integrated into the workplace, plus a host of changes are brought about by remaining competitive in the global marketplace and the continuous search to improve.

Teamwork Atrophies without Constant Attention. Like the proverbial rose garden that grows weeds when unattended, people systems degenerate into a state of disrepair without consistent use. When that happens,

- Walls go up between departments.
- Employees replace helping each other with griping, complaining, and moaning.
- Leaders quit creating the environment that encourages their employees to participate and communicate at high levels of proficiency.
- Morale plummets as do production and profitability.
- The TeamWork Values Statement goes into the trash-can.

The interesting question is, why does this automatic degeneration occur? The bottom line is that it's nature's way. That which is not used atrophies. Life is full of such examples.

- Couch potatoes gain weight and their muscles weaken while watching television.
- A car not driven or a house not lived in quickly begins to deteriorate.
- A prolonged illness that results in being bed-ridden weakens the muscles.
- Equipment not used begins to rust.
- An athlete who quits exercising quickly gets out of shape.
- An unattended garden quickly grows weeds.

Consider what happens when the living organism does not successfully move forward. Animals become extinct. People derail their careers. Organizations die. Many proud companies that were once included among the elite—the *Fortune* 500—no longer exist.

Perhaps Howard Schultz says it best in his book, *Pour Your Heart into It: How Starbucks Built a Company One Cup at a Time.*

We are seldom motivated to seek self-renewal when we're successful. When things are going well, when the fans are cheering, why change a winning formula?

The simple answer is this: Because the world is changing. Every year, customers' needs and tastes change. The competition heats up. Employees change. Managers change. Shareholders change. Nothing can stay the same forever, in business or in life, and counting on the status quo can only lead to grief.

Survival of the Fittest. The psychological message communicated here is "taking care of oneself—if I don't take care of me, no one will and I will perish." Not necessarily the attitude for effective working relationships, is it?

But the survival-of-the-fittest attitude sticks its ugly head up in the workplace whenever an individual attempts to win at the expense of others:

- Taking credit when it is due elsewhere.
- My idea is better than your idea.
- Sabotaging the success of others through communicating false information and other means.

Survival and protecting oneself are basic instincts and powerful emotional drives. The survival instinct may have its place on the golf course or tennis court, but working in an organization is a team sport. The organization's survival depends upon people working together, not competing with each other.

Normal Wear and Tear. Even with proper maintenance, equipment breaks down—that is, components quit cooperating with each other. Without maintenance, the toll of wear and tear occurs more rapidly.

Without proper rest and nourishment, our bodies break down. The body is simply not made to withstand chronic use or abuse.

The same happens with teamwork. The organizational wear and tear of day-to-day operations and the alligators biting at your posterior eventually take their toll, and the Team-Work Values Statement is temporarily forgotten. Emotional outbursts occur, cooperation is lost, and working relationships are adversely affected.

The Path of Least Resistance. Like flowing water, people tend to take the path that requires the least effort. Work and putting forth energy are required to help others to be more successful. Easy ways out include:

- Withholding information rather than keeping others informed.

- Focusing on a personal agenda rather than encouraging others to express their ideas or listen to understand them.

- Expressing anger rather than remaining emotionally calm.

Asking people to participate in something new is like stretching a rubber band. As long as you hold both ends, the rubber band remains stretched. When the path of least resistance (that is, you get tired of holding the stretched rubber band) encourages you to release it, the rubber band quickly returns to its original state. When you grow tired of practicing teamwork, the progress quickly deteriorates.

Systems to the Rescue

Systems are tools, and those organizational leaders who recognize human capital as their most important asset realize the advantages associated with the systematic use of the people systems to develop their people asset.

1. *Order from Chaos.* We've discussed the chaos that would exist if every department were allowed to develop its own reporting systems for finances, production, and so on. As a result, we realize the importance of standard procedures. Obviously confusion is not conducive to success. Adopting a systems approach instills order. This order is reflected in knowing where you want the organization to go via the definition of the TeamWork Values Statement and the performance system components to hold teamwork accountable. These two criteria are vital to leading your organization into the future. The systematic approach to develop people capital leads to a high-performing and profitable company more so than allowing it to occur by chance. Yes, a blind hog will eventually find an acorn, but in today's marketplace you need to capitalize

upon every advantage to build a profitable company rather than relying on blind luck.

2. *Make the Process Permanent.* Employees often wonder if these new people systems are temporary or a permanent process. Employees have seen many ideas come and go, and they naturally wonder if the people systems will be one of those forty-eight-hour fads.

Seeing is the antidote for believing in this case. The systematic schedule to measure and put the data to work throughout the organization sends the message that people systems are here to stay. This point is key. Systems drive a behavior change, and a permanent installation of the performance management system detailed in this book can continue to drive improved teamwork. Like the rubber band mentioned in the preceding section, teamwork deteriorates if you stop using the systems.

We need to remember that diamonds were once pieces of coal. This same persistence can move your organization into the people age and make people believe that working relationships are more valuable than diamonds.

3. *Develop People Assets.* The core of a successful business is successful people working together. People systems guide the continued development of people and their working relationships. A systematic approach with a defined purpose to improve people performance and working relationships demonstrates that the importance of developing people capital is equal to developing technical capital.

4. *Convert Words into Behaviors.* The importance of workplace interpersonal skills is no secret. Any employee in any organization can tell you about the positive and negative impact that interpersonal behaviors have upon morale and productivity. A systems approach has two critical components. One is a structure to encourage using the behaviors contained within the TeamWork Values Statement in the day-to-day operations. Second is a system to continually improve interpersonal performance and teamwork while documenting success through measurement.

5. *Orient New Employees.* The typical procedure to help new employees get off to a fast start is to provide a thorough orientation about the organization. Until now this description has focused on the technical characteristics: vision and mission statements, products/services, policies and procedures, and messages from the corporate leader(s). Now the orientation can include a thorough explanation of the teamwork culture and the associated people systems.

New employees experience a tremendous advantage when they know the people side of the organization rather than relying on the typical rumor mill and learning the personalities of their organization's leaders by trial and error. Now new employees can study the desired corporate culture being implemented.

We've jokingly suggested in seminars about publishing a manual to be read by new employees during the orientation period listing the strengths and weaknesses of the organization's leaders and what each is doing to improve their personal performance. That is not going to be done, because of potential embarrassment. In reality, people's strengths and weaknesses become public information anyway through the rumor mill that fills the ears of new employees. The public commitment of the leaders to improve their performance would send a very powerful message to new employees about the significance of the teamwork culture.

6. *Retain Employees.* Put quite simply, which company would you prefer working with: one that says "I don't care about employees" or "I care about employees"?

7. *Right Thing to Do.* Now is the right time to take care of the asset that takes care of the organization, because it is simply the right thing to do. You regularly schedule changing your automobile's oil, because it is the right thing to do to promote your car's health. If your car oil is left unattended, major motor problems can result, costing you money. People drive the organization's engine. People left unattended can likewise cost your company money. It just makes sense to take care of the asset that takes care of the company.

Ending with a Success Story

The September 20, 1999, issue of *Industry Week* listed "Managing with heart" as one of the attributes that drive successful organizations. The article described the people culture at Manco, led by Jack Kahl, to illustrate the impact of people taking care of people on their financial bottom line, while capturing over 60 percent of the duct tape market with its Duck Tape brand.

To begin with, everyone in the organization is described as a partner and has a name tag with their first name written in large letters. Partners know about the progress of the company through an array of charts describing the company goals, progress, and monthly profit or loss statements.

Partners are encouraged to thank other partners for their contributions by sending thank-you notes and through other means. Celebrating a public thank-you is a frequent occurrence at staff meetings. The culture institutionalizes the process of showing partners appreciation for jobs well done, because caring for people boosts both morale and productivity.

Another strong feature of the reported culture is that honesty is the rule rather than the exception. Managers hold meetings and provide answers to dispel rumors. The company's internal newsletter emphasizes the importance of giving nothing but honest answers.

In Closing

The behavior exhibited by Manco's employees stretched the organization and created a culture that was described as simply having fun! If Manco's employees stopped exhibiting their systems and behaviors, the organization would lose those characteristics that underlie having fun and high performance. If you stop implementing the systems outlined in this book, your organization would likewise regress back to its original state. Using a systems approach to develop your people capital can help you build a competitive advantage and keep you there.

15 | The Workplace Is the University for Personal Development

Any industry always has an elite group of organizations that outperform their competitors, and for whom your employees may wish they worked. Such organizations, in general, are truly interested in providing a humane workplace environment, in helping people to work more efficiently, in improving morale, and in assuring that all team members have the opportunity for continuous personal development. James Collins and Jerry Porras mention several of these companies in their best-selling book *Built to Last:* Ford Motor Company, Disney, Motorola and IBM. Moreover, Daniel Goleman does the same in his best-selling book *Working with Emotional Intelligence:* American Express and Nokia Telecommunications Group.

The leaders of these companies recognize that great organizational accomplishments are the result of people accomplishing great things, and they are committed to creating a work environment in which personal excellence becomes the rule rather than the exception. We've introduced the concept of a systematic process to develop your people capital and your people operating system. The focus of this chapter is to use the TeamWork Values Statement as your guide to improve interpersonal effectiveness. The three themes we discuss are as follows:

- Continued personal development.
- Organizing training processes and quantifying behavior change.
- Teaching the value statement and using the workplace environment as the natural classroom.

The TeamWork Values Statement Is Your Personal Development Course

Consider the workplace environment as the University of Interpersonal Development, enabling you to learn effective interpersonal skills. Every working day you confront disappointments, frustrations, and discouragement while working with multiple persons and their personalities. To put it simply, the workplace is a rich tapestry of learning opportunities to maximize your personal effectiveness while working with uncomfortable events and people.

Taking advantage of these day-to-day frustrations requires that you exhibit a commitment to your personal excellence. You must not only demonstrate a willingness to use your TeamWork Values Statement, but also institutionalize it as your personal development course. To do so means putting several essential ingredients to work for you that we've previously discussed. First are the five windows, discussed in chapter 13, to continuously learn about yourself and to be open to receiving the necessary feedback that guides your commitment to improve interpersonal performances. For instance, volunteer to participate in a multi-rater procedure to obtain feedback about the perceived use of the behaviors contained in your TeamWork Values Statement. Doing so can be as simple as asking your coworkers to rate your use of the behavioral characteristics using the traditional paper-pencil methodology or electronically, as with the MBC Software®. If for some reason that is not possible, then by all means use the values statement as a self-assessment tool and honestly evaluate your use of these behaviors. You want to be recognized as a model of excellence, so develop a personal development plan to continuously improve your interpersonal performance. Then incorporate the seven-step personal change process that we detailed in chapter 11.

Classroom Training

Training on people skills has received a bad rap, in part because these skills are oblique and subjective in nature. The major complaint is the inability to quantify the behaviors recently introduced into your behavioral repertoire. Consequently, organizations find it difficult to fund these types of development programs. Perhaps Goleman states it best in *Working with Emotional Intelligence:* "[O]nly about 10 percent of the training results in a behavior change, so millions upon millions of dollars are being wasted on training programs that have no lasting impact or little effect at all. . . . It amounts to a billion-dollar mistake." The looming question is "What is contributing to the billion-dollar mistake?" Is it the quality of the instructor, the course content, an unwilling student, or the lack of organizational support to drive a behavior change? The traditional approaches to training on people skills contain an element of humor, because organizational leaders would not dare to approach training on technical issues in the haphazard manner in which training on interpersonal behaviors is completed.

1. *Hit-or-Miss Mentality.* We cannot tell you the number of times we've been asked about the value of sending employees to one of the traveling seminars. What happens is an advertising brochure with a catchy marketing title lands on a desk, and the person sitting behind the desk thinks, *This is just what we need.* The truth of the matter is that you can pick up good ideas from attending such seminars. The challenge

is how to put your newly acquired knowledge to work—how to turn ideas into action when only one or at best a few of the employees have received the training.

2. *Organizational Leadership.* Organizational leaders also have a tremendous impact on whether training is converted into a behavior change in the workplace. While conducting a seminar on the topic of organization and cultural changes, several participants from one company announced, "There is no way we would be allowed to do what you are teaching," and promptly left the seminar.

Let's return to our "I Don't Care" company to consider another question. Suppose an employee from this company attends a seminar on how to motivate employees through empowerment, encouraging them to express ideas and extending positive recognition for a job well done. What is the likelihood the organization's culture will support these new behaviors?

The existing "I Don't Care" culture has an immunity system to attack any foreign substance that might threaten the status quo of its comfort zone. Unless an organizational effort is made to change the culture, the existing "I Don't Care" culture will beat the devil out of the individual's attempt to implement the newly acquired behaviors to motivate employees. The obtained knowledge then atrophies as the result of not being used. Subsequently the training gets a bad rap from the corporate soothsayers, when in reality the training had virtually no opportunity to be successful. Sending people to a training session makes no sense if the culture is unlikely to support the new set of behaviors.

3. *Say One Thing and Do Something Else.* A sad and humorous corporate practice is trying to act as if the employees are trained to perform a particular set of interpersonal skills when they are not.

A friend visited a well-known fast-food chain after 10:00 p.m. A sign on the window said, "No bill larger than a twenty can be accepted after 10:00 p.m.," but the lady at the service window was proudly wearing an "Our employees are empowered!" button. My friend decided to test the empowerment process and gave the attendant a one-hundred-dollar bill, which she promptly returned with the statement, "I'm sorry, sir. I can't accept any bill larger than a twenty."

He asked about the empowerment button and pleaded with her to use that authority. She continued to insist that she could not. My friend asked to see the manager. He explained to the manager that the employee is supposed to be empowered and yet could not accept the one-hundred-dollar bill, to which the manager replied, "That's correct. The company policy dictates that we do not accept any bill larger than a twenty after 10 p.m." My friend asked about the empowerment button. The manager said, "Sir, these showed up at our store with a memo to ensure that every employee wore one. We still can't accept that bill at this hour."

My friend asked the employee what she thought about the empowerment process, to which she quickly replied, "Sir, quite frankly I think it stinks!"

Our bank, unfortunately, provided us with another example. Our original bank had been purchased by a larger bank, which touted itself as customer service gurus, because of the wealth of resources they provide to their customers. As you know, a financial service institution uses customer service as the flag to differentiate itself from its competitors. We asked for and received a small credit line. Our first draw constituted about 50 percent of that line. But immediately, we began receiving notices for payment that indicated we had received 90 percent of the loan amount. We worked with that procedure for about four months before it was corrected. During that time, we received multiple telephone calls about our delinquent payment, even though each time we explained that no payment would be made until the correction was made.

During the last six weeks, some conversations became cantankerous. For instance, one person told us that many of the banks were just upset they had been purchased and were making the merger extremely difficult for everyone. Another employee called us and wanted to know what our problem was, and we explained that our problem was their records. This lady was so disrespectful that we eventually talked to her supervisor (who had promised to call us on several occasions, but we had to continue to call her). Then when we finally made contact, there was never an apology for the bank's error and she defended her employee's behavior by telling us that "she was having multiple family problems and she was allowing them to affect her work."

The bottom line was that all the beautiful words about customer service were just empty promises. Our local branch continued to be embarrassed about the entire ordeal and the "I don't care" corporate attitude.

4. *Lack of Accountability.* How many times have you heard, "It is a waste of our time to participate in that team-work training, because nothing is going to change anyway"? The lack of accountability or structure to facilitate the use of the behaviors in the workplace environment (including not using an effective measurement system) is often the culprit that allows the training sessions to degenerate into an exercise in futility.

Learning from the Technical Track

For just a moment, let's contrast training on people skills with the focused training associated with the technical track. Suppose an individual is hired to serve as a computer technician. For discussion purposes, let's also suppose the employee lacks a particular skill to complete the job responsibilities. No problem. He or she can be trained in that knowledge area to fill the deficit. Or consider the training associated with equipment changes. For example, a company purchased a state-of-the-art color printing press; naturally, several days of training were scheduled so press operators could learn how to operate the new equipment. Purchasing the equipment and not training employees on its use would be ridiculous.

As you know, ongoing training is imperative in our fast-changing technical world; otherwise, the knowledge and skills quickly become antiquated. The point being addressed is that the training to support the technical track of the business is focused and organized to maximize use of resources. No random hit-or-miss training methodology is employed here.

The question we are posing in this chapter is, "Why are we not applying the same level of common sense to implement training to develop the people assets?" The process to organize an ongoing training program to support the desired people culture and measure its impact can be achieved to maximize the return on the financial investment to conduct the training process. That is simply a good business decision.

Maximizing Return on Your Training Financial Investment

The first step to maximize the return on your training investment is to ensure that all training on interpersonal skills and teamwork is designed to support the creation of the culture described in the TeamWork Values Statement. When training is delivered, the participants need to know what specific behaviors and values contained within your value statement are being strengthened. In other words, participants need to know the training on interpersonal skills is just as focused and meaningful as is the training completed to improve their performance on their technical responsibilities. To illustrate how training can be organized to support the desired culture, we use the four behavioral values and their behavioral definitions that are frequently contained in the company's TeamWork Values Statement, and we list suggested training topics. You can certainly add to this list.

COOPERATION

Definition and Training Topics
1. Understand each other's needs.
   A. Active listening.

    B. Organizing and expressing yourself.
2. Willingly help each other.
    A. Cross-training technical responsibilities.
    B. Personal motivation to be a high performer.
3. Solve problems in a win/win manner.
    A. Conflict resolution.
    B. Scientific problem-solving process.
    C. Negotiating skills
4. Competently complete job responsibilities.
    A. Personal motivation to be a high performer.

COMMUNICATION

Definition and Training Topics
1. Encourage the expression of ideas.
    A. Assertiveness.
    B. Organizing and expressing yourself.
2. Listen to understand each other's needs.
    A. Active listening to understand.
3. Honestly presenting the facts.
    A. Assertiveness.
4. Keep each other informed.
    A. Communicate effectively with the different work styles.
    B. Determine the necessary information to be kept informed.
5. Receive feedback regarding job performance.
    A. Coaching/teaching.

RESPECT

Definition and Training Topics
1. Listen to understand each other's needs.
    A. Active listening.

2. Use each other's ideas whenever possible.

   A. Self-esteem and self-confidence.

3. Accept each other as individuals.

   A. Diversity.

4. Care about each other's feelings.

   A. Interpersonal skills.

   B. Diversity.

5. Everyone is equally important.

   A. Diversity.

   B. Consistent application of policies and procedures.

TRUST

Definition and Training Topics

1. Dependable and do what we say we will do.

   A. Strategic planning and goal setting.

   B. Accountability.

2. Confidential information is kept confidential.

   A. The importance of remaining silent with confidential information.

3. Authority is delegated to the lowest level.

   A. Delegation/empowerment.

4. Allowed to do our job.

   A. Delegation/empowerment.

   B. Coaching/teaching.

The training bottom line is that all interpersonal development is designed to promote the institutionalization of the culture described in your TeamWork Values Statement.

Accountability through Measuring Behavior Change

"Does the training on people skills transfer from the classroom to the workplace environment?" has been an ongoing question. D. L. Kirkpatrick offered a four-tiered measurement in 1975 in an effort to create a model to answer this daunting question. We do not intend for the following discussion to provide a complete thesis on the issues associated with measuring behavior change attributed to training, nor to imply that Kirkpatrick is the only model available for measuring behavior. Our intent is to show that you can measure transfer of learning. Kirkpatrick suggested the following four measurement levels.

Level 1: Measuring the student's reaction to the program upon its completion. This is largely a popularity measurement in terms of how well the students liked the course content and the instruction.

Level 2: Measuring the attitude, knowledge, and behaviors learned as the result of the program. The student would be asked which behavior is s/he going to use in the workplace environment.

Level 3: The student and others measuring the extent to which the behaviors taught in the classroom are being used in the workplace environment.

Level 4: Measuring the business impact of the program through improved quality, costs, time and/or customer satisfaction.

Up until recently, the predominant measurement processes have relied on Levels 1 and 2, because of the ease of use. The measurement process that we introduced in this book provides the technology to obtain Level 3 and Level 4 measurements. That is, you can determine if the behaviors taught in the classroom are being used in the workplace environment.

Let's revisit the example of training operators on the new color printing press. Two methods are available to assess the success of the technical training. The first is to watch the operator run the press; the second is to analyze the quality of the finished product. Seeing the behavior change produced by technical training is relatively simple.

Contrast the relative ease of seeing technical changes with the question, "How do you know whether training in any of the people skills mentioned here results in changes that benefit your organization?" Actually, you have the same two opportunities to assess changes in people skills in the workplace that you do with regard to implementing technical change. You can watch the new behavior being implemented; you can also measure the result—in this case, the degree to which the new behavior is being used.

You can see the student use the behavior while in the classroom, but it is more of a challenge for the up-line supervisor to observe the behavioral change in the workplace environment. That is, you can't predict when the student has the opportunity to use the new behavior, so it is not practical for the up-line supervisor to wait around and see the application of the behavior. Measuring the use of the behavior allows you to see the behavioral change.

Measuring also provides you the opportunity to focus additional attention on any behavior that did not transfer. Behavioral solutions can be defined to strengthen these behaviors and measure their implementation.

Remember, we advocate an open learning environment that allows up-line supervisors to review down-line data, thereby taking advantage of the accountability systems discussed in chapter 11. In addition, the up-line supervisor has the opportunity to provide supplementary coaching or other support that might be required to improve performance.

The training community is also presented with another challenge, as highlighted in Jack Phillips's book *Return on Investment*. Phillips added a fifth level of measurement to more accurately compute the return on investment. He suggests computing the costs of the training program and determining the financial impact of the training to gauge the actual return on investment of the training program.

Phillips further points out that calculating a return on investment is certainly easier to complete when the training event focused on technical knowledge, sales, and customer service than the impact of training on the more abstract interpersonal behaviors such as trust, respect, and communication. For example, how do you measure the financial impact of an investment to conduct training that encourages individuals to express their ideas without fear of reprisal upon production? This question leads to an interesting controversy regarding the capability of measuring the impact of people skills training upon technical performance.

Ron Zemke, editor of *Training,* has questioned the validity of doing so, because there are so many extraneous variables impacting technical performance that it is virtually impossible to isolate the specific impact associated with training on people skills. Our intent is to bring this information to your attention, as resolving this dilemma is beyond the scope of this book. We simply want you to know that you can use data to answer the question, "Does training on people skills improve interpersonal performance?"

Leaders Are Teachers

Many people accept leadership positions without realizing that doing so is synonymous with entering the teaching profession. The traditional course/seminar format continues to provide excellent opportunities for sensitizing people and training them in the relevant social skills. However, the most important step during training transfer involves using the natural work environment as a classroom to learn and practice using your people skills. Teaching and training is an everyday, all-day-long occurrence, with work unit leaders providing the leadership and support to create an open environment conducive to learning.

Once again, let's consider the technical side of training and transfer. What does a leader do upon seeing one of his or her employees incorrectly apply a procedure while completing one's technical responsibilities? The leader assumes the role of a teacher and corrects the individual. It is absolutely ridiculous to allow the individual to continually repeat the error. The important point is that this instruction occurs in real time and, more importantly, in the natural work environment.

Now, let us switch back to the training and transfer of people skills to the work environment. What happens when a work unit leader observes a team member causing frustration in working relationships? Let's answer that question with an example. While working with an organization, we were discussing an employee's attitude and behavior with the work unit leader. In short, the employee gave the appearance that "he knew everything there was to know and being here was a waste of his time." The leader agreed with the observation and explained to us that this employee was his "problem child." Upon being asked what is being done to improve this individual's performance, the leader responded, "Nothing now. I discussed his behaviors with him a couple of times without success, and he is such a high technical performer that we are simply putting up with it. Everyone knows he is difficult to work with."

A typical procedure that really sends chills down one's back is to listen to a work unit leader note that s/he documents the incidents to be discussed during the next formal performance review. Months could pass between the incidents and that discussion. The employee in question may have forgotten them by then. Even if he had not, the impact is certainly less than if discussed at the time of the incident.

Stop-and-Think Model

The time to enter the people age is now. We can do better, and it is time to do better. We think you'll agree that the following easy-to-use-coaching model can help turn the workplace into the natural classroom.

George Bache, Ph.D., and Howie Knoff, Ph.D., introduced this very useful model to us. These two school psychologists developed this model to teach children the necessary self-discipline to use effective interpersonal skills. We're facing the identical challenge with adults in the workplace, so the model created for kids can also be used with kids in adult clothing.

Let's introduce the basic components of the model, and then we discuss each in more detail.

An Incident Occurs.

Tell yourself to "Stop & Think!"

Do you want to make a good choice or bad choice?

What are the good choices?   What are the bad choices?

1. _____   1. _____
2. _____   2. _____

What are the consequences associated with good and bad choices?

Which good choice are you implementing?

The good choices are defined via your TeamWork Values Statement. Suppose, for example, your TeamWork Values Statement includes the statement, "remaining emotionally calm." Let's further suppose a frustrating incident occurs in the workplace, and you observe an individual who loses his/her emotional control and displays behaviors that include griping, complaining, and finger-pointing. Obviously, such behaviors are not consistent with the value statement.

Implementing this model allows you to very sincerely remind the person of the need to "Stop and Think." Or you may also ask the individual, "Do you want to make a good choice or bad choice?" This very effective and easy-to-use model allows you to coach individuals by emphasizing the desired and expected behavior in a socially acceptable manner.

Using Stop & Think and the Seven-Step Personal Change Process

Step 1: Recognize the Need to Change. Using this model can help people to more fully understand the consequences associated with making good or bad choices as they participate in the brainstorming sessions used to define the consequences. For example, the disadvantages associated with losing emotional control could include

- Showing others your inability to successfully cope with frustrating situations. (Obviously, this is not effective personal marketing behavior.)
- Saying words you later regret.
- Damaging the working relationship with others.
- Acquiring the reputation of being a hothead.

Recognizing the need to change is based on the disadvantages exceeding the advantages associated with losing control and listing the advantages, which could be

- Venting and the release of emotional energy, which allows you to feel better.
- Providing the energy to be assertive to express feelings that may otherwise be left unsaid.

Step 2: Accept Responsibility. The objective is to help the individual understand that the behavior is his/her choice and is not caused by another person or situation. In this phase, review the choices the individual has when the event occurs that typically results in their loss of emotional control—that is, the good and bad choices.

Step 3: Know the Desired Behavior. The desired behavior emerges from the discussion about the choices available at the time the emotion-provoking incident occurs. The good choice obviously represents the desired behavior.

Step 4: Being Willing to Change. Willingness to change is based on the advantages of the good choice exceeding the advantages of the bad choice. The advantages of remaining emotionally calm can include

- Maintaining effective working relationships.
- Feeling better, thus promoting both physical and emotional health.

- Remaining logical, thus saving time by allowing you to more quickly enter into a problem-solving process to determine the next steps.
- Capitalizing on yet another opportunity to practice remaining in control during a difficult situation, which increases this behavior's habit strength.

Obviously, the employee must recognize that these advantages are more "advantageous" than those associated with losing emotional control.

Step 5: Personal Image. After processing the above information, the pertinent question is, "The next time this situation or a similar one occurs, what will be the decision?" The desired answer: to remain emotionally calm. A follow-up question would be, "Do you see yourself being able to remain emotionally calm in this situation?" Getting inside the employee's head to see the real image of the performance would be nice, but since that's not possible, the best you can do is to ask and then observe their behavior. Their behavior will ultimately tell you what they see.

Step 6: Practicing Behavior. Schedule several role-playing scenarios with the employee to practice the good choice or desired behavior. Perfect practice makes for perfection, but the real test occurs in the natural classroom—the workplace.

Step 7: Offering Feedback. The objective is to help the employee acquire personal control of the behavior and to make good choices. Doing so requires immediate feedback from you, the supervisor. When the good choice is selected, provide positive recognition. When the bad choice is selected, ask the employee to consider a good choice. As quickly as possible, revert to Step 6 and practice another role-playing scenario with the specific incident that resulted in the employee making the bad choice. If you should happen to be present at the time the incident occurs, you may have the opportunity to ask the employee if he/she wants to make a good or bad choice, which can help the individual remain in control.

Speaking of anger and remaining emotionally calm, the following information was received in an email, and we thought you might find it interesting if you have not already read it.

There once was a little boy who had a bad temper. His father gave him a bag of nails and told him that every time he lost his temper, he must hammer a nail into the back of the fence. The first day the boy had driven thirty-seven nails into the fence. Over the next few weeks, as he learned to control his anger, the number of nails gradually dwindled down. He discovered it was easier to hold his temper than to drive those nails into the fence.

Finally the day came when the boy didn't lose his temper at all. He told his father about it, and the father suggested that the boy now pull out one nail for each day that he was able to hold his temper. The days passed and the young boy was finally able to tell his father that all the nails were gone.

The father took his son by the hand and led him to the fence. He said, "You have done well, my son, but look at the holes in the fence. The fence will never be the same. When you say things in anger, they leave a scar just like this one. You can put a knife in a man and draw it out. It won't matter how many times you say you are sorry, the wound is still there."

A verbal wound is as bad as a physical one. Friends are a very rare jewel indeed. They make you smile and encourage you to succeed. They lend an ear, they share words of praise, and they always want to open their hearts to us.

In Closing

Organizational synergy is created when individual pieces work in synchronization with each other. Using the TeamWork Values Statement to both define your teamwork culture and as the organizing principle for your ongoing training process can create synergy as the people track of your organization is aligned to drive your organization's technical and financial success.

16 | Now You Have It, What Are You Going to Do with It?

You have just completed reading about a comprehensive system to develop your people and their working relationships. The question to be answered is, "What are you going to do with this knowledge?" Is this going to be another one of those books that was read and put in your library? Are you going to recommend that others in your organization read it to obtain additional reactions? Are you going to put this book to work for you?

One of the greatest challenges in the corporate community is to establish the necessary momentum for organizational leaders to systematically develop their most valuable asset: their people and associated working relationships. Too frequently we hear employees say, "We say the words about being committed to the development of our people, offer some training courses, and even complete an employee survey every year or so, but we don't do anything more." Or we hear many senior-level organizational leaders state, "We would like to do something to improve teamwork, but we just don't seem to have the time."

We hope you agree that such behaviors are corporate tragedies. It would be interesting to know the loss of human potential because of such thinking, although that figure can never be calculated, which is probably just as well because it could send all of us into a state of depression. It's sad to say, but people are the victims of such thinking.

Opening the Door into the People Age

We've sprinkled examples of people-age thinking throughout this book to both show and encourage you to enter the door and begin capitalizing upon the unlimited potential resting within your employees. It has been estimated that a million square feet would be required to hold the computer that is as powerful as the three pounds of gray matter located between the ears. Assuming that 10 percent of this potential is being used and another 10 percent is dead because of abuse, that still leaves eight hundred thousand square feet to be developed. Now you do the math with the number of your employees, and look at the potential resting within your corporate halls. Surprising when you look at it from this perspective, isn't it? What would happen if we could just squeeze another 1 or 2 percent from each individual?

Yes, organizations exist to generate profits for their stakeholders, and people working together generate those profits. Those companies that systematically work to improve people performance have a decided advantage over those that don't, and they are capitalizing on an interesting human phenomenon: People want to be happy. We challenge you to examine when you are the happiest. We not talking about being belly-laughing happy, although that too is important for emotional and physical health. We are talking about satisfied happy. Our guess is that such a feeling occurs when you are creating something, when you are using your personal resources to produce something.

Organizations need to serve as a means for people to create themselves. Quite frankly, we believe that being a university for development is a primary reason for an organization to exist. That is, the workplace provides the opportunities for employees to continuously improve both their technical and interpersonal skills. The challenge for organizational leaders is to create the workplace environment so that their employees are challenged to use more of their human potential, or to create themselves. Doing so increases personal happiness that leads to higher performance. Higher performance can lead to higher profits.

Systems Allow You to Enter into the People Age

We have tried to convince you that maximizing human potential requires a systematic, orderly process just as maximizing your manufacturing or service delivery requires a systematic process. Confusion and chaos exists in the absence of systematic processes. These behavioral attributes are not going to bring you to where you want to be.

Maximizing people capital means to unleash the people potential walking within your corporate hallways and to improve individual performance within the three working relationships composing your people operating system. By now you know that doing so requires the systematic application of the four major components of the teamwork system. At the risk of being redundant, we end this book listing these components:

1. Write the TeamWork Values Statement detailing the desired values and behaviors to institutionalize these values.
2. Quantify the as-is situation to identify strengths and opportunities to improve individual performance or the working relationships.
3. Develop, implement, and measure the impact of the behavioral solutions designed to improve the measured weaknesses.

4. Monitor the people operating systems data on an on-going scheduled basis.

As you know, accountability or doing what is expected is a key factor leading to successful organizational change. In the words of Ralph Waldo Emerson, "What you do speaks so loudly, I can't hear what you say." Now can be the time to convert your words into action. In addition to talking about the importance of maximizing people performance, you now have the blueprint to do it.

In Closing

The decision to enter the people age is yours.

About the Authors

Larry Cole, Ph.D., founded TeamMax®, Inc. in 1989 and the TeamMax® methodologies that are designed to improve people's performance in the people operating systems to maximize financial success.

He is cofounder of PeopleSystems SoftWare, Inc. and created the MBC Software® methodology, which is pioneering the measurement of values-based working relationships and leadership.

He has authored three books, including the first book published in the poultry industry on the subject of improving working relationships between a poultry company and its contract growers. Additionally, he has written over forty articles on personal and organizational development.

Each year Larry speaks to thousands of people on personal development, implementing change, and measuring teamwork. He can be contacted at:

TeamMax®, Inc.
5 East Towering Pines
Conway, AR 72032
800-880-1728 (Voice)
lcole@cei.net (email)
www.teammax.net
www.people-systems.com

Michael S. Cole, Ph.D., is a Senior Research Fellow and Lecturer at the University of St. Gallen, located in Switzerland. His interests revolve around the design and application of research designs to organizational and personnel problems, such as personnel selection/placement and assessments of the readiness for organizational change. As an author, he has published more than thirty articles in academic and practitioner-related journals.

He is also involved in a longitudinal research project with several participating companies located throughout Europe, Asia, and the United States. The purpose of this research consortium is to determine the drivers and focusing variables that influence personal and organizational energy. Michael can be contacted at:

University of St. Gallen
Institute for Leadership and HR Management
Dufourstrasse 48
CH - 9000
St. Gallen, Switzerland
011+41/071/224 2378 (Voice)
Michael.Cole@unisg.ch (email)

INDEX